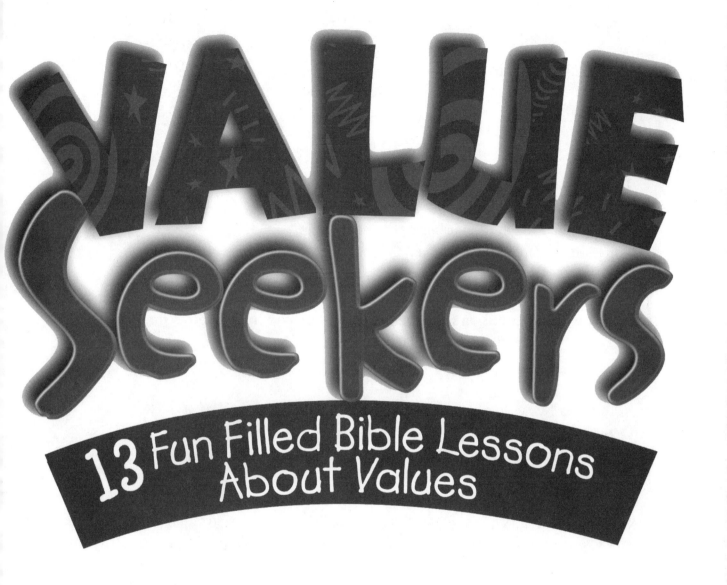

VALUE Seekers

13 Fun Filled Bible Lessons About Values

Susan L. Lingo

Standard PUBLISHING

CINCINNATI, OHIO

DEDICATION

**Seek first his kingdom and his righteousness,
and all these things will be given to you as well.
Matthew 6:33**

Value Seekers
© 2000 Susan L. Lingo

Published by Standard Publishing, Cincinnati, Ohio
A division of Standex International Corporation

Credits

Produced by Susan L. Lingo, Bright Ideas Books™
Cover design by Diana Walters
Illustrated by Marilynn G. Barr and Megan E. Jeffery

08 07 06 05 04   5 4
ISBN 0-7847-1145-3
Printed in the United States of America

CONTENTS

SECTION 1: TRUTH & HONESTY

SECTION 2: LOVE & KINDNESS

SECTION 3: THANKFULNESS & PRAISE

SECTION 4: FORGIVENESS & CHANGE

VALUE SEEKERS REVIEW LESSON

INTRODUCTION

POWERING UP YOUR KIDS' FAITH!

Congratulations! You're about to embark on a wonderful mission to strengthen, energize, and stabilize your kids' faith and fundamental knowledge of God—faith and fundamentals that will launch your kids powerfully into the twenty-first century!

Value Seekers is part of the Power Builders Series, an exciting and powerfully effective curriculum that includes *Faith Finders, Servant Leaders, Disciple Makers,* and *Value Seekers,* the book you're now holding.

Value Seekers is dedicated to exploring a wealth of Christian values that God desires us to have so we can serve and live in today's—and tomorrow's—world. Thirteen theme-oriented lessons will help your kids explore, assess, and apply values such as truth, honesty, love, kindness, forgiveness, change, thanksgiving, and praise. In addition, woven throughout each lesson is Scripture, Scripture, and more Scripture!

Each lesson in *Value Seekers* has the following features:

POWER FOCUS (Approximate time: 10 minutes)—You'll begin with a mighty motivator to get kids thinking about the focus of the lesson. This may include an eye-popping devotion, a simple game, or another lively attention-getting tool. Included is interactive discussion and a brief overview of what kids will be learning during the lesson. *Purpose: To focus attention and cue kids in to what they'll be learning during the lesson.*

MIGHTY MESSAGE (Approximate time: 15 minutes)—This is the body of the lesson and includes engaging Bible passages that actively teach about the lesson's theme. The Mighty Message is not just "another Bible story," so your kids will discover God's truths through powerful passages and important portions of Scripture that are supported by additional verses and made relevant to kids' lives. Processing questions help kids explore each side of the passages and their relation to the theme, beginning with easier questions for young children and ending with more challenging think-about-it questions for older kids. Meaty and memorable, this lesson section will help kids learn tremendous truths! *Purpose: To teach powerful biblical truths and offer thought-provoking discussion in age-appropriate ways.*

MESSAGE IN MOTION (Approximate time: 10-15 minutes)—This section contains engaging activities that enrich and reinforce the lesson theme. It may include creative crafts, lively games and relays, action songs and rhythmic raps, mini service projects, and much more. *Purpose: To enrich learning in memorable and fun ways that build a sense of community.*

SUPER SCRIPTURE (Approximate time: 10-15 minutes)—This all-important section encourages and helps kids effectively learn, understand, and apply God's Word in their lives. The Mighty Memory Verse was chosen so every child can effectively learn it during the course of three weeks, but an extra-challenge verse is offered for older kids or children who can handle learning more verses. You are free to substitute your own choice of verses in this section, but please keep in mind that the activities, songs, crafts, and mnemonic devices are designed for the Mighty Memory Verse and the accompanying extra-challenge verse. And remember, when it comes to learning God's Word, effective learning takes place when kids work on only one or two verses over the course of several weeks! *Purpose: To memorize, learn, recall, and use God's Word.*

POWERFUL PROMISE (Approximate time: 5-10 minutes)—The lesson closes with a summary, a promise, and a prayer. You'll summarize the lesson, the Mighty Memory Verse, and the theme, then challenge kids to make a special commitment to God for the coming week. The commitments are theme-related and give kids a chance to put their faith into action. Finally, a brief prayer and responsive farewell blessing end the lesson. *Purpose: To make a commitment of faith to God and express thanks and praise to him.*

POWER PAGE! (Take-home paper)—Each lesson ends with a fun-to-do take-along page that encourages kids to keep the learning going at home. Scripture puzzles, crafts, recipes, games, Bible read-about-its, Mighty Memory Verse reinforcement, and more challenge kids through independent discovery and learning fun. *Purpose: To reinforce, review, and enrich the day's lesson and the Mighty Memory Verse.*

PLUS, in every Power Builder's book you'll discover these great features!

★ **WHIZ QUIZZES!** At the end of each section is a reproducible Whiz Quiz to gently, yet effectively, assess what has been learned. Completed by kids in about five minutes at the end of lessons 3, 6, 9, and 12, the Whiz Quiz is a nonthreatening and fun measuring tool to allow teachers, kids, and parents to actually see what has been learned in the prior weeks. When kids complete each Whiz Quiz, consider presenting them a collectible surprise such as measuring cups that represent how they can measure the growth and learning they've accomplished for God. For example, after the first Whiz Quiz, present each child with a ¼-cup measuring cup. After the next Whiz Quiz, present ⅓-cup measuring cups. Then use ½- and 1-cup measuring cups for lessons 9 and 12. When the book is complete, kids will have a whole set of measuring cups on which they can write "Measuring up for God!" (one word on each cup). Kids will love the cool reminders of the lessons and their accomplishments! Be sure to keep children's completed Whiz Quiz pages in folders to present to kids at the end of the book or at the end of the year, in combination with other Whiz Quizzes from different books in the Power Builders Series.

★ **LESSON 13 REVIEW!** The last lesson in *Value Seekers* is an important review of all that's been learned, applied, accomplished, and achieved during the past twelve weeks. Kids will love the lively review games, action songs, unique review tools, and celebratory feel of this special lesson!

★ **SCRIPTURE STRIPS!** At the back of the book, you'll discover every Mighty Memory Verse and extra-challenge verse that appears in *Value Seekers*. These reproducible Scripture strips can be copied and cut apart to use over and over for crafts, games, cards, bookmarks, and other fun and fabulous "you-name-its"! Try gluing these strips to long Formica chips to make colorful, clattery key chains that double as super Scripture reviews!

★ **TEACHER FEATURE!** Discover timeless teaching tips and hints, hands-on help, and a whole lot more in this mini teacher workshop. Every book in the Power Builders series offers a unique Teacher Feature that helps leaders understand and teach through issues such as discipline, prayer, Scripture memory, and more. The Teacher Feature in *Value Seekers* is "Dealing With Discipline."

God bless you as you teach with patience, love, and this powerful resource to help launch kids into another century of love, learning, and serving God! More POWER to you!

DEALING WITH DISCIPLINE

**Where'er I may roam, by field or by pool—
I'll always remember my sweet Sabbath school!**

Ahh, memories of sweet Sunday school, with lessons to learn, verses to recite, picturesque picnics on soft summer days, and dealing with discipline. Dealing with discipline? If your memories are those of a Sunday school teacher, they no doubt include memories of Miss Stubborn, who never wanted to help clean up, or Mr. Chatterbox, who chatted his way through every quiet moment.

We've all had kids like this in class, right? We love them, but they can also be frustrating and challenging! How can we help them stay on track and focus on God? What can we do to nurture their self-esteem while maintaining firm guidelines against intruding on others' right to learn and have fun? And how can we correct without negative confrontations?

Dealing with discipline isn't easy, but there are ways to emerge through it healthy, happy, and whole—for both kids and teachers! This mini workshop is designed to give you valuable insights into discipline, how you react to kids in different situations, and what you can do right now to help create a warm, loving classroom that encourages and engages all kids in gentle, yet effective ways. But first, let's do a quick assessment of you as a teacher! Ready?

★ How do I view children?

★ What do I expect from my children?

★ Am I into structure or control? principles or rules?

★ What is my goal as a Sunday school teacher?

Believe it or not, the answers to these simple questions may reveal hidden agendas that are so veiled we don't even know they exist! Since our ultimate goal is a healthy environment for kids, it's imperative that adult expectations, viewpoints, and goals are consistent, realistic, and healthy. But many teachers seem to operate from a set of unrealistic expectations that either set their kids up for failure or themselves up for grave disappointment.

According to Dr. Becky Bailey in *There's Gotta Be a Better Way*, there are three main philosophies guiding interaction between teachers and children, and whichever philosophy you choose defines how you deal with discipline. Read through each to see which one most closely resembles the way you respond to children in your own classroom. They are enlightening!

Punitive Guidance System. The goal of this approach is unquestioning obedience to those in authority. Teachers believe that rules must be obeyed at all costs. There is little give and take on rules, and rules are generally set up by the teacher. Summary: The teacher wants to be the "boss." Down side: may squelch independent thinking and reasoning.

Permissive Guidance System. This strategy seeks to remove all discomforts for children. Teachers believe that if they are fun, nice, and lively enough, all kids will naturally behave. There is quite a bit of give and take on rules, which are usually made by the children and not always upheld by the teacher. Summary: The teacher wants to be everyone's "best friend." Down side: confusing expectations with little or no motivation and challenge.

Responsibility Guidance System. The goal of this system is children who are creative, responsible, and make healthy choices while thinking of others. There is give and take on rules, which are generally principle-based and set up by the children with guidance from the teacher. Summary: The teacher wants to be the "facilitator." Down side: a bit more patience and planning is required.

Did you see yourself mirrored in any of these strategies? Each has unique ways of dealing with problems and searching for resolutions. Which is best? Let's look to the Bible for the answer! Jesus advocated and embodied love, forgiveness, nonjudgmental attitudes, and choice—but certainly not without consequences. Punitive discipline tends to be judgmental in a subjective way (the teacher's way!), and although a teacher may be loving, choice and respect are often removed from children in the name of control. On the other hand, permissive discipline is really an oxymoron, isn't it? How can you discipline children who have already had their way? Permissive discipline tends to be haphazard and wishy-washy, giving kids freedom without accountability. But responsibility-based discipline emphasizes healthy choices with appropriate consequences for wrong decisions—which is very biblical! And responsibility-based discipline focuses on forgiveness and respect without judgment.

Responsibility-oriented discipline also stresses principle-based guidelines for behavior instead of rule-based edicts. Teachers help kids develop their own guidelines for classroom behavior, and "rules" are founded on Christ-centered principles such as, "Treat others as you want to be treated," "Forgive others," and "Help each other." That way, if a child is speaking out and disturbing others, a gentle reminder to help others by not being disruptive stresses a positive principle and accomplishes much more than just saying, "Please be quiet!"

Choices are an important feature of responsibility-based discipline. Instead of using a heavy-handed approach to guide kids into positive behavior, allow children the freedom to choose their behaviors, but hold them accountable for their decisions—and look for great teachable moments! For example, if a child decides to hit another child, point out that this is not a choice Jesus would make and have the child sit in a time-out area until she apologizes. Then encourage the other child to make a good decision to forgive the wrong-doer. By setting limits through choices and consistently following through when wrong decisions are made, kids will learn responsibility for their actions and words as they become more autonomous and aware of the consequences of their choices.

We've briefly covered three philosophies that influence how you deal with discipline and have hopefully established that responsibility-based discipline is a healthy choice for teaching kids. It's appropriate that the word *discipline* comes from the word *disciple*, which means "one who is taught." Effective discipline techniques will teach kids about themselves, others, God, the choices we all face, and the consequences of our choices. So let's get down to the real nitty-gritty so we can get on PAR with this discipline thing! That's PAR as in Prevent, Act, and Resolve—the three-step approach to solving any classroom crisis!

PREVENT! Preventing discipline problems before they arise is so much easier than dealing with them when they've become full blown! Know your kids and how they'll react to situations. If you have chatters, seat them beside quieter kids. If you have frustrated or inattentive kids, a gentle finger on the shoulder will keep them focused when they begin to "wander." And kids who are aggressive may respond to being given extra responsibilities in the classroom, such as being your special messenger or helping another child as his partner-pal. Look for creative ways to defuse problems before they explode. Remember: an ounce of prevention is worth a pound of cure.

ACT! Once a problem arises, be sure kids are kept safe from any physical outlashes. When a child is physically aggressive, separate him with a firm reminder that you want to help resolve the dispute but that hitting, pushing, or other physical acts will not be tolerated. Don't be afraid to use a time-out or cooling-down area. If the problem is between two children, guide them to their own conclusions about what happened and how this problem can be resolved. Asking the favorite question, "What would Jesus do?" goes a long way in giving kids powerful insights into their own and others' behaviors. If the problem is between you and the child, don't get into a match of wills—you will lose and so will the child. Calmly discuss the issue at hand and be sure to listen to the child's thoughts before the two of you decide on a resolution.

RESOLVE! Go ahead, let the peacemaker in you flow! Resolving disputes is the most powerful part of discipline because it allows kids to see mistakes, make good choices, experience forgiveness, and change. In fact, the object of resolution is change without resentment or anger. It's a logical conclusion to a problem, but not necessarily a conclusion without consequences. Time and again the Bible tells of consequences that God sets forth, consequences that are just yet loving. Matthew 6:14, 15, for example, reminds us of the reward for being forgiving and the consequences of being unforgiving. Help kids be accountable and responsible for their choices in behavior and words, just as we're accountable in every other area of our lives. Remind children that resolving problems isn't about winning or losing—it's about learning and forgiving!

Finally, here are a few tried 'n true ideas that might make dealing with discipline easier for you and decision-making a bit easier for your kids. May God bless you as you continue your powerful—and patient—ministry with kids!

★ **STOP THAT POP!** (Hebrews 10:24)—Fill six helium balloons and divide them into two groups of three. Explain that each time a group or someone in that group displays negative behavior (give examples), you'll pop a balloon. Point out that each group has three chances and that at the end of the day, week, or month any group with at least one balloon can choose a favorite game or some other positive reward. If both groups have balloons left, have a party!

★ **FORGIVENESS JELLY BEANS** (Matthew 6:14, 15)—Fill an interestingly shaped jar with colorful jelly beans. Explain that when someone asks for forgiveness or you want to ask for forgiveness, simply present that person with a jelly bean. This idea helps "break the ice" for kids needing to ask for forgiveness and encourages them to seek it in a nonthreatening way.

★ **SMILE AWHILE GOOD-BYES** (Ephesians 4:26)—Cut out a pile of bright neon circles and draw happy faces on them. If there has been a problem between you and a child or between two children and you notice that the anger or hurt hasn't subsided when it's time to leave, hand each of the parties involved a happy face with the reminder that God doesn't want the sun to go down on our anger or hurt. Encourage kids to smile and shake hands, then tell them you'll look forward to seeing them next week.

TRUTH & HONESTY

Therefore love
truth and peace.
Zechariah 8:19

THAT'S THE TRUTH!

God's Word is true.

Psalm 19:7-11
2 Timothy 3:15-17

SESSION SUPPLIES

★ Bibles
★ construction paper
★ fine-tipped markers
★ two brown paper grocery bags
★ several yards of yellow ribbon
★ a birthday candle for each child
★ scissors, tape, pencils
★ photocopies of the What It Is and What It Does handout (page 123)
★ photocopies of the Power Page! (page 19)

MIGHTY MEMORY VERSE

Your word is a lamp to my feet and a light for my path. Psalm 119:105

SESSION OBJECTIVES

During this session, children will
★ discover that the Bible is the inspired Word of God
★ explore God's Word in the Bible
★ learn that God is trustworthy
★ understand that God's Word guides us to be truthful

BIBLE BACKGROUND

Who wrote the Bible? Is it true? How long did it take to write the Bible? Are God's words really applicable to my life? These are the most commonly asked questions about the Bible. Scholars have argued over how many people and years it took to record God's inspirations. Theologians have disputed about which are the best manuscripts and most original texts. Even lay people have debated about the best Bible versions for life application. But the one subject that scholars, theologians, and lay people agree on is that God's Word is true and guides our lives when we obey it.

Psalm 19:7-11 is a descriptive and powerful passage about the life-changing power of God's Word. From these five verses, we learn the fullness of what God's Word is as well as what it does for us. Perfect and trustworthy, right and radiant, pure and sure—verses 7-10 say that God's

Word is all of these. Verse 11, on the other hand, tells us about the inner joy and great reward that those who obey God's statutes experience. Help children recognize, understand, and value the power of Scripture with this lesson aimed at the Bible and God's truth.

POWER FOCUS

Before class, prepare a special bag by cutting the side from one grocery sack and taping it to the inside of the other paper bag to make a secret pocket. (See illustration.) Slide a pencil, a paper heart, a piece of ribbon, and a birthday candle into the secret pocket.

Gather kids and hold up the paper bag containing the hidden items. (Be sure to hold the top of the secret pocket closed so the items don't escape!) Quickly show kids the inside and outside of the bag and say: **This looks like a pretty ordinary paper bag, doesn't it? But did you know there are really lots of useful things inside? Let's see what surprises we have.** Push the secret pocket open and pull out the items one by one. Encourage kids to explain why each is useful, then set the items on a table and fold the paper sack. Hold up the Bible and say: **The Bible looks like an ordinary book, but just like our paper bag, there are lots of wonderful and useful surprises in the Bible—maybe some you didn't know were there!**

Point to each of the items from the paper bag as you say: **Just as a ribbon ties things together, the Bible shows us how to stay close to God. Pencils help when we need to remember important things, and God's Word helps us remember important truths in life. How are a birthday candle and a heart represented by the Bible?**

Allow children to tell their ideas, then say: **There are so many wonderful, useful, life-giving truths in the Bible, but do you know the best part? The Bible is true! The Bible is God's Word, and his Word is always true. Listen to what God's Word does for us.** Read aloud 2 Timothy 3:15-17. Then say: **And that's just some of what God's Word will do for us! Today we're going to learn more about God's Word and how it teaches us to be truthful in all we do. Along the way, we'll also discover how God's Word is a lamp to our feet and a special light to our paths!**

THE MIGHTY MESSAGE

Ask children to tell what an author is and how authors use pencils, computers, or even typewriters to write books. Then hold up the Bible and say: **God is the most famous and wisest author of all time. God wanted his ideas, rules, and wisdom put into a book so people could learn from his Word. So God helped people put down these truths into the book we know as the Bible.** Ask:

★ **Why do you think God wanted to give us the Bible?**

★ **How does the Bible reveal God's love for us?**

★ **What kinds of things can we learn from the Bible?**

Say: **The Bible teaches us how to live the way God wants us to live, and the Bible guides our lives with love and wisdom. Let's read from the Bible. Listen carefully to all that God's Word is and does.**

Read aloud Psalm 19:7-11, then read each verse again, one at a time, and ask children to point out what God's Word is and what it does for us. Then ask:

★ **In what ways does God's Word guide us?**

★ **How does God's Word warn us?**

★ **Why is it wise to obey God's Word?**

Hand out pencils and the What It Is and What It Does handouts. Have kids form pairs and, using Psalm 19:7-9, fill in the answers in the correct outlines. For example, for verse 7 children will write "perfect" on a space in the Bible outline and "revives the soul" on a space in the heart outline.

When the outlines are complete, have each pair join another pair and compare their lists. Then say: **The Bible is the inspired Word of God and is true, trustworthy, right, radiant, pure, and sure. God's Word warns us, gives us joy, makes us wise, gives us light, and guides us in being truthful. God's Word is a lamp to our feet and a light to our paths. In other words, God's Word guides us! Let's play a game to discover more about how God's Word guides us down perfect paths.** Set the pencils and handouts aside until later.

POWER POINTERS

Children often ask, "Are there any mistakes in the Bible?" Remind kids that God makes no mistakes but that people who read the Bible sometimes forget or confuse small details.

THE MESSAGE IN **MOTION**

Place the paper bag in the center of the floor and hand each child a birthday candle. Form four teams and have each team stand five feet from and on opposite sides of the bag, like compass points. Explain that in this relay race, one person from each team will close his eyes, walk backward to the paper bag, and drop his candle in the bag. If a player misses the bag, he should pick up the candle and try again. When a candle is in the bag, the player walks backward to his team so the next person can go. When all the candles on a team have been deposited in the bag, have the team sit in place.

When all teams are finished, repeat the race, but this time have team members find partners to guide them to the bag. Helping partners can walk forward with their eyes open and help guide their partners. Have kids switch roles until all the candles have been dropped in the bag.

When the relay is over, ask:

★ **Which was easier: walking with or without your partner? Explain.**

★ **How is this like going through life with God's Word to guide us?**

★ **Why is it important to rely on God's guidance?**

Say: **When we're walking blindly and are unsure of the path, the trip is difficult. But when someone guides us, we can move smoothly, with trust and assurance. That's how it is with God's Word. God's Word is a powerful guide to help us stay on the path God sets before us. Now let's use your candles to learn a Mighty Memory Verse about God's Word.**

SUPER SCRIPTURE

Before class, cut an 8-inch piece of yellow ribbon for each child. If you would like, photocopy the Scripture strip for Psalm 119:105 from page 126 for kids to tape to one end of their ribbons.

Have children form pairs or trios and hand each child a yellow ribbon to use as a special bookmark. Say: **Our Mighty Memory Verse for this month is Psalm 119:105. Open your Bibles in the middle and find Psalm 119:105.** Help children find the verse as needed, then invite three volunteers to each read the verse aloud as kids follow along.

Say: **This is such a powerful verse! I can almost see the lamp for my feet and the light for my path, can't you? But what does this verse mean?** Allow children to share their ideas, then say: **This verse says that**

God's Word guides us. It gives us the light of God's wisdom to show us where to go and what to do and say. Think for a moment. If we tried to walk down a path in the dark, what might happen? We might get hurt or become lost or even afraid! But if we have a light to guide our feet on the path, we feel secure and know where we're going. God's Word is a powerful light that guides us—and we can trust God to help us find the path to him. God's Word is a lamp to our feet and a light for our path! Ask:

★ In what ways does God's Word help us? protect us? warn us?

★ How can you rely more on God's Word every day?

Say: **We need to know what God's Word says. Then we want to understand what God means. And finally, we can put God's Word to use in our lives by being truthful! These ribbon bookmarks are yellow to remind us of the light of God's Word. Use these markers to write "Psalm 119:105" on your ribbon.** Let children use fine-tipped markers to write the Scripture reference. Encourage kids to keep the bookmarks in the correct place in their Bibles and challenge them to review the verse often during the week.

Lead children in repeating the Mighty Memory Verse three more times, then say: **Let's make neat reminders of this Mighty Memory Verse. We'll make colorful pictures to help us remember the words, and your candles can represent the word "light" in the verse.**

Have children make simple construction-paper Bibles (to represent God's Word), lamps, footprints, and paths. (Use the illustration to guide you as needed.) Tape varying lengths of yellow ribbon to the shapes and to the candles, then suspend the items from tightly rolled construction-paper tubes. Add a long length of yellow ribbon to each paper tube so it can be suspended. When the Memory Mobiles are complete, challenge kids to see if they can repeat the Mighty Memory Verse by looking at the pictures. Then repeat the verse three times in unison.

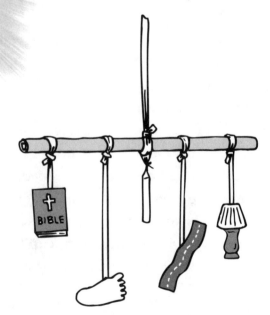

Invite children to help hang the Memory Mobiles around the room, then say: **God's Word is true and trustworthy, and his Word guides us in every part of our lives. Let's thank God for his perfect Word with a special promise and a prayer.**

A **POWERFUL** PROMISE

Have kids sit in a circle and ask for a moment of silence, then hold up a birthday candle. Say: **A birthday candle gives us a bit of light when it's lit. But God's Word is a much more special light! God's Word is a light that shines brightly with truth and shows us the right way to live. We've learned today that God's Word is true, and we've discovered that the Bible is God's inspired Word and useful for every part of our lives. We've also worked on the Mighty Memory Verse that says,** (pause and encourage kids to repeat the verse with you) **"Your word is a lamp to my feet and a light for my path."**

Hold up the Bible and say: **God promises that his Word will always be true. Let's make a promise of our own to God. We can each commit to reading a few verses from the Bible every night this week. If you open your Bible in the middle like this, you'll be in the book of Psalms. Read several verses from Psalms every night this week and think about how good and true**  **God's Word is. As we pass the Bible around the circle, we can make our own special promises and thank God for his Word. We can say, "Thank you for your Word, God. I want to read it every day."** Pass the Bible until everyone has had a chance to thank God.

Have kids hold their What It Is and What It Does handouts. Form two groups and designate one the What It Is group and the other the What It Does group.

Say: **Let's end by reading what God's Word is and what God's Word does from our lists. The What It Is group will read aloud their first word, then the What It Does group will respond with what God's Word** does for us. For example, group one will say, "God's Word is perfect," and group two will say, "It revives the soul."

When both lists have been read, end with a corporate "amen." Then say: **Hang your paper in a place where you'll see it often and remember that God's Word is true and given to us with love.** End with this responsive good-bye:

Leader: **May God's truth be with you.**

Children: **And also with you!**

Distribute the Power Page! take-home papers as kids are leaving. Thank children for coming and encourage them to keep their promises to read the Bible this week.

POWER PAGE!

Unscramble the words that describe God's Word! Use Psalm 19:7–11 to help you.

uetr _____   yturstrowth _____

girht _____   dinarta _____

repu _____   sreu _____

HIGH-n-LOW

Use Psalm 119:105 to fill in the high and low letters to the verse.

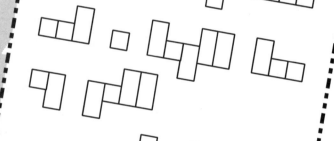

119:105

BIBLE LIGHTS

The Bible tells us that God's Word is a light. Look up the verses below and write or draw other types of light found in the Bible.

Psalm 19:4

Matthew 2:2

Matthew 25:1

John 8:12

TRUE FREEDOM

Jesus is the truth that sets us free.

John 8:31, 32; 14:6

SESSION SUPPLIES

★ Bibles
★ a box of letter envelopes
★ scissors and markers
★ rubber bands
★ newsprint and tape
★ photocopies of the paper doll on page 124
★ photocopies of Psalm 119:105 and 104 (page 126)
★ photocopies of the Power Page! (page 27)

MIGHTY MEMORY VERSE

Your word is a lamp to my feet and a light for my path. Psalm 119:105

(For older kids, add in Psalm 119:104: "I gain understanding from your precepts; therefore I hate every wrong path.")

SESSION OBJECTIVES

During this session, children will
★ recognize that lying is a sin that holds us captive
★ discover that Jesus is the truth
★ learn that Jesus' love and forgiveness set us free
★ explore how Jesus' example in God's Word helps us remain in the truth

BIBLE BACKGROUND

Chains and slavery were all too common during biblical times. From the Israelite slavery in Egypt to Peter and Paul being wrapped in chains and locked in jail cells for their devotion to Christ, being held captive meant not only a loss of physical freedom but also being kept from doing God's work. Captivity did not always involve chains and prison cells, however. It was also a part of our spiritual lives before Jesus Christ came as the truth that sets us free, breaking the chains of sin and death. With the truth that Jesus brought, spiritual freedom was born and physical death died.

Kids often feel invisible chains of their own. Small lies turn into the proverbial "downhill snowballs" and may soon run out of control in a child's heart and mind. What do I do? they wonder. Kids need to learn the truth about the truth: that Jesus is the truth who sets us free from sin, dishonesty, and the deceitful tangles that ensnare our spirits and keep us far from God. This lesson helps kids understand that valuing Christ and his truth is the only sure way to be free—and that's the truth!

POWER FOCUS

Before class, prepare and practice this cool attention-grabber. Photocopy and slightly enlarge the paper doll pattern on page 124. Make a copy for each child and one extra. Color and cut out one doll. Draw a happy face on one side and a sad face on the other. Seal an envelope, then cut off the two short ends. Cut two slits in opposite ends of the back of the envelope, but don't cut through to the front! Slide the paper doll down into the envelope from the top opening. As the doll slides down, guide it through the slits in the back of the envelope so its head and feet stick out the top and bottom of the envelope.

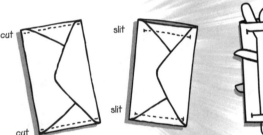

At the appropriate time, simply snip across the envelope to make it look as though you're cutting through the doll. (Since the doll is in the back slits, you won't really be cutting it!) Hold the envelope together and set the scissors down. Quickly pull the paper doll out of the envelope halves and show your children the uncut doll—they'll be amazed!

To begin, gather kids and place the scissors and envelope containing the paper doll beside you. Have kids stand with their feet together and their arms tightly against their sides. Ask them to hop in place, touch their toes, then clap. (Of course they won't be able to do everything!) Then say: **This is what it must be like to be held captive in chains. You can't move freely or even be comfortable. It would feel pretty awful to be held in chains all the time, wouldn't it? Today we'll be learning about dishonesty and how it keeps us chained and feeling bad. We'll also learn about the only way to be set free! But first, there's someone I'd like you to meet.**

Have kids sit down, then hold up the envelope containing the paper doll. Be sure the sad face is facing the kids. Say: **This is Joe. Ooo, he's very sad today—do you know why? Yesterday Joe did something dishonest. He used the lunch money his mother gave him to buy candy on the way to school. Then he told his teacher he forgot his lunch. And when his mom asked how lunch was, Joe said it was great and so nutritious! Now Joe feels bad about all his dishonest words and deeds. Have you ever felt like this after doing something dishonest?**

Pause for kids to tell their thoughts, then continue: **Joe feels trapped and awful by what he did. In fact, all sin makes us feel trapped in a terrible way. How can Joe be set free? How can he feel at peace with God again?** Pause for kids' responses, then snip through the envelope and free the paper doll as you say: **There is someone who can set us free and keep us in truth and on the right path to God! Jesus can set us free!**

Hold up the uncut paper doll with the happy side facing the kids. Say: **In fact, the Bible tells us that Jesus is the truth that sets us free. What do you think that means?** Encourage children to share their ideas, then say: **Jesus is the truth—and he also helps us be truthful. And that's something to smile about! See? Even Joe is happy! Today we'll learn more about Jesus being the truth that sets us free. But first let's see what the Bible teaches us about Jesus being the truth, the whole truth, and nothing but the truth!**

POWER POINTERS

Help kids understand that Jesus is the truth by telling them the letters stand for "the real uplift to heaven"—that it's only through Jesus' truth that we're able to live with God in heaven.

THE MIGHTY MESSAGE

Say: **Last week we learned that God's Word is truth and guides us on the right path to God. Today let's explore how Jesus teaches that he is the truth that sets us free. Stand up and link elbows. As I read the Bible passages, gently tug to try and free yourselves. Then when you hear what can set us free, drop elbows and shout, "Free at last!"** Read aloud John 8:31, 32. After kids drop elbows and shout, have them sit in a circle and read John 8:34, 36. Then ask:

★ **Who is the truth that sets us free?**

★ **In what ways can truth free us from the slavery of sin and deceit?**

★ **How can we receive Jesus' true freedom? In other words, how can we allow Jesus to set us free?**

Say: **When we know, love, and follow Jesus, he sets us free from being trapped by sin, deceit, and dishonesty. Isn't that wonderful? Jesus tells us he can set us free, and Jesus also tells us why: because he is the truth. Listen as I read John 14:6.** Read aloud the verse, then ask:

★ **In what ways is Jesus the truth?**

★ **How does being free from sin bring us closer to Jesus? to God? to others?**

Say: **When we follow Jesus' example of truth and love, we can't be dishonest. In John 8:31 and 32, Jesus tells us that if we follow his teaching we will know the truth. How can we follow Jesus and learn more about what he teaches so we can know the whole truth?**

Allow kids to tell their ideas, which might include reading the Bible, being kind to others, praying, and being honest. Then say: **Being truthful starts in the heart and comes out in our words and our behavior. And Jesus helps us remain in the truth when we love and accept him into our lives! Ahh, what freedom! We can help bring that freedom to others, too. We can teach them about Jesus being the truth and about how Jesus sets us free. Let's learn how to make our own Freedom Dolls to teach others the truth about Jesus.**

THE MESSAGE IN MOTION

Have kids form small groups and hand each child an envelope and a paper doll. Have kids color their paper dolls on both sides and make one face happy and the other sad. Then demonstrate how to prepare the envelopes and how to slide the paper dolls between the slits.

When kids finish, have them use their envelopes to present the devotion in their groups, cutting through the envelopes to free the paper dolls. Encourage them to use statements such as, "When we lie and cheat, we become trapped by sin. But Jesus is the truth that sets us free!"

When everyone has had an opportunity to present the devotion in a small group, ask:

★ Why do we want others to learn about Jesus being the truth?

★ How can we teach others about the truth? about how Jesus sets us free?

★ Who is one person you can tell about the truth this week?

Say: **We can feel happy knowing we have the truth about the truth! We know that God wants us to be truthful. We know that Jesus is the truth. And we know that Jesus sets us free from sin! Let's each tell someone this week the truth about the truth!**

Hand each child another envelope to take home to present this devotion to families and friends.

SUPER SCRIPTURE

Before class, photocopy and cut apart Psalm 119:105 from page 126. If you want an extra challenge for older children, copy and cut apart Psalm 119:104, too. Cut the verses into puzzle pieces so that when they're reassembled, the verse can be read. Place each set of puzzle pieces in an envelope. Prepare one envelope for every two kids.

Form pairs and hand each pair a rubber band and an envelope containing the Scripture puzzle pieces. Have kids place the envelopes on the floor and sit beside them. Instruct partners to place the rubber band around one of each of their wrists and to place their other hands behind their backs.

Say: **We've been learning that dishonesty can keep us trapped and that Jesus is the truth that sets us free. While you're trapped and able to use only one set of hands, reassemble the Mighty Memory Verse puzzle in your envelopes. When the puzzle is reassembled, read it aloud, then set yourselves free as you shout, "Jesus is the truth that sets us free!"** (Kids using verses 104 and 105 will have two verses to assemble before they are set free.)

When all the verses have been reassembled, read them aloud in unison two times, then say: **God's Word is true, and we can learn so much about the truth from the Bible. We discover that Jesus is the truth, and we also find that Jesus is the light.** Read aloud John 12:46, then ask:

★ **In what ways is Jesus a light?**

★ **Why are the words *light* and *truth* good words to describe Jesus?**

★ **How can staying in Jesus' light help reveal truth to us?**

★ **Why is it important to help others have the light of Jesus' love? of God's Word?**

Say: **Jesus is the truth and the light. And just as our Mighty
Memory Verse says, our path is lit by special light—the light of
God's Word and the light of Jesus' truth! We can use God's Word as a
lamp to our feet in walking toward God, and we can use God's Word
as a light for our paths in staying on the path of truth with Jesus.
With God's Word, we learn about what is true and can avoid deceit
and dishonesty. Wouldn't it be great if everyone knew the truth
about the truth? Let's share a special prayer and promise about
helping others know about the real truth Jesus offers!**

A POWERFUL PROMISE

Before class, write the words to "The Truth About the Truth" responsive
rhyme on page 26 on two sheets of newsprint, labeling one sheet card 1 and
the other card 2. Tape the newsprint to the wall.

Have kids sit in a circle and ask for a moment of silence. Then quietly say:
**We've learned today that Jesus is the truth that sets us free and that if
we know, love, and follow Jesus, we remain in the truth and the truth is
in us. We've also discovered that Jesus is the light that brings light and
truth to the world. And we've reviewed the Mighty Memory Verse that
says,** (pause and encourage kids to repeat the verse with you) **"Your word is
a lamp to my feet and a light for my path."** (Also repeat verse 104 with
older kids.)

Hold up the Bible and say: **We're so blessed to know the truth about the
truth, aren't we? And we can help others know that truth, too. Let's
each commit to telling one person the truth about the truth this week.
If you'd like, you can use your doll
devotion to help. As we pass the Bible
around the circle, we can make our
own special promises. We can say, "I
want to tell the truth about the truth."**

Pass the Bible until everyone has had a
chance to hold the Bible. Then share a
prayer thanking God for his Word that is
true, for Jesus who is the truth that sets
us free, and for helping us live honest
lives before God. End with a corporate
"amen."

Form two groups and say: **Let's end our time with a fun "truth about the truth" rhyme. This group will repeat the words on card 1** (point to the words), **and this group will respond with the words on card 2** (point to the words). **We'll repeat the response two times and then switch sides.** Have kids rhythmically repeat the words on the newsprint so one group answers the first group. If you can get a little loud, kids will love it! After repeating the verses twice, switch groups and repeat the rhyme two more times. For more fun, encourage kids to invent actions to accompany the words, such as clapping hands, snapping fingers, or stomping feet.

THE TRUTH ABOUT THE TRUTH

(Card 1)

Tell me now, the truth about the truth!
Tell me now, the truth about the truth!
Tell me now, the truth about the truth—I want to know!

(Card 2)

The truth is . . .
God's Word is true and always will be!
We can be truthful to God, you and me!
Jesus is the truth with a capital T—
JESUS IS THE TRUTH THAT SETS US FREE!

Distribute the Power Page! take-home papers as kids are leaving. Thank kids for coming and encourage them to keep their promises to tell others the truth about the truth this week.

POWER PAGE!

TRUTH TREASURES

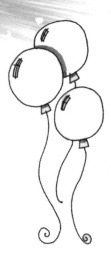

You'll need: slips of paper, a pen, ribbon or string, and seven uninflated balloons.

Directions: On each slip of paper, write one sentence about Jesus, God, or the Bible. Fold each slip of paper and slide it through the open end of a balloon. Blow up the balloons and tie them in knots. Use ribbon or string to tie all the balloons together and place the bouncy bouquet by the dinner table. Each night at dinner, choose a balloon and pop it, then read the sentence aloud and discuss what it means with your family.

Honesty IS the Best Policy!

Did you know that some people in the Bible were dishonest with God? Read more about how each person fibbed and found out that HONESTY TO GOD IS THE BEST POLICY!

☐ Genesis 3:1-19   ☐ 1 Samuel 15:1-23   ☐ Acts 5:1-10

**Fill in the missing words to Psalm 119:105.
Then list three ways God's Word lights YOUR life!**

_____ word ___ a _____ to ___ _____ and __
_____ ___ my _____ . (Psalm 119:105)

1. _____
2. _____
3. _____

HONEST TO GOD

We can be truthful
to God, others, and
ourselves.

1 John 3:18, 20-22
Leviticus 19:11

SESSION SUPPLIES

★ Bibles
★ several long twigs
★ rolls of clear tape and
   markers
★ a paint stir stick for each
   child (available free at paint
   stores)
★ crepe paper
★ a large men's handkerchief
★ several toothpicks
★ photocopies of the Whiz
   Quiz (page 36) and the
   Power Page! (page 35)

MIGHTY MEMORY VERSE

Your word is a lamp to my feet and a light for my path.
Psalm 119:105

(For older kids, add in Psalm 119:104: "I gain understand-
ing from your precepts; therefore I hate every wrong path.")

SESSION OBJECTIVES

During this session, children will
★ learn that truth and honesty start in the heart
★ discover the importance of being honest
★ realize that truth and trust are related
★ understand that being truthful is a way to honor God

BIBLE BACKGROUND

Honesty has literally been at the heart of people's relationship with God from the very beginning of time, when God
trusted Adam and Eve to respect and obey him. Dishonesty
starts in our hearts, and if we're not walking closely with
God and living by his example of truth, we may fall away, as
did Adam and Eve. Other biblical men and women strove for
honest obedience to God, in their dealings with others, and
with themselves. David was honest with God and himself
when he finally realized his sin with Bathsheba. Solomon
was honest with others as he ruled Israel with truth and wisdom. And those who weren't honest with God and others,
such as Ananias and Saphira, learned harsh lessons in obedience and truth at God's hand.

First John 3:18, 20b-22 is a powerful passage that enlightens us to nurturing an honest relationship with God, others, and ourselves. Children will relate to this teachable passage from their own early experiences with truth and deceit as well as the feelings of guilt associated with lies and the peace that a truthful heart brings. Help children learn more about the value of truth and honesty as you explore why God wants us to be truthful and what blessings come from an honest heart!

POWER FOCUS

Before class, sew or glue a narrow hem along one side of a men's handkerchief. Leave the ends of the hem open so a toothpick (or piece of uncooked spaghetti) can be slipped inside and hidden. During the Power Focus presentation, you'll cover one toothpick with the hankie and hold it in one hand as you hold the hidden toothpick inside the hem in the other hand. Have a child break the toothpick that is inside the hem (it will appear to be the covered toothpick that's broken). When the covered toothpick is revealed—voilà—it will be as whole and unbroken as our word should be! (Keep the broken toothpick in the hem until kids leave.) Practice this slick trick several times before class.

To begin, be sure one of the toothpicks is hidden in the hankie hem. Gather kids and hold up the other toothpick. Ask kids what toothpicks are used for, then say: **Toothpicks can come in handy for many things, like getting out food that's caught in our teeth or cleaning in tiny places. But if a toothpick is broken, it's not much good anymore. That's a lot like it is with truth and honesty. We can pretend this toothpick stands for truth and honesty. It's good and solid unless we cover up the truth.** (Cover the toothpick with the hankie and hold it in one hand. Position the hidden toothpick in your hand so it's the one that will be broken in a moment!) **What are things that cover up the truth?**

As kids mention things such as lies, cheating, stealing, and other dishonest acts, have them break the toothpick that's secretly hidden in the hem. Then say: **Lies and other dishonest things not only cover up the truth, they** break it! And not being truthful hurts God, others, and even ourselves. When we're dishonest, no one believes what we say or do! So what does God want us to do? (Uncover the whole toothpick and hold it up.) God wants us to keep the truth whole and unbroken to him, to others, and to ourselves, too. Honesty and truthfulness begin inside our hearts with how we feel and how we love God. Today we'll learn more about the importance of being truthful to God and others, and we'll discover how great we feel when we're truthful with ourselves as well! Now let's see what the Bible says about being truthful and honest and how God helps us.

THE **MIGHTY** MESSAGE

Gather kids and ask them to tell about times they might have lied or cheated and how they felt afterward. Then say: **When we're not truthful in what we say and do, it makes us feel pretty awful. We might feel guilty, sad, ashamed, or even angry. God knows how wrong it is to tell lies, to cheat, and to act dishonestly—and he knows how it hurts us inside.**

POWER POINTERS

Kids sometimes think that telling a "white lie" is okay. Remind them that God wants us to be honest in both our words and deeds and that no lie is a good one—white or otherwise!

When we're dishonest to friends and other people, we're being dishonest to God and ourselves as well. God sets a powerful example by always being truthful, and that's how God wants us to be. In other words, we can be truthful to God, others, and ourselves. Honesty starts in our hearts and with loving God and wanting to follow his example of truth and honesty! Listen to what God's Word says about being truthful. Read aloud 1 John 3:18, 20b-22 and Leviticus 19:11, then ask:

★ **Who should we be true to? Why?**

★ **Why should our actions be as truthful as our words?**

★ **What things happen when we lie, steal, cheat, or act dishonestly?**

★ **What good things happen when we're truthful and honest?**

Say: **Remember the story of the boy who cried wolf? He lied so many times that, when he finally told the truth, no one believed him. That's** pretty sad, isn't it? It's so important to be truthful and honest in all we say and do. That way, others can trust us and we feel good going before God. Like the Bible says, we feel at peace before God when we're truthful. God knows all we think, do, and feel—and he knows when we're not truthful. Adam and Eve were dishonest when they ate the forbidden fruit and tried to hide from God. But God knew they had been dishonest, and it made him very sad. God knows when we're truthful and act honestly, too—and it makes him so happy when we don't break our word! Let's play a game to see what happens when we break the truth one too many times.

THE MESSAGE IN **MOTION**

Place two twigs at one end of the room. Form four groups and have them form four lines at the opposite end of the room. Designate two groups the Breakers and two the Tapers. Hand the first person in each Tapers line a roll of tape. Explain that in this lively relay, two Breakers and two Tapers will hop to the twigs. The Breakers will each break a twig and the Tapers will tape them together again. Have kids hop back to their lines and four more kids go. Continue until everyone has had at least one turn to break or tape a twig. When everyone has had a turn, sit in a circle and hold up the twigs. Ask:

★ **How easy was it to break the twigs? How hard was it to repair them?**

★ **Are the twigs as good as before they were broken? Explain.**

★ **How is this like truth once it has been broken? like our promises? like our word?**

Say: **These twigs aren't as good as new. They're not as strong as before they were broken. Did you know that when we break the truth to God and others, after a while no one believes us? We want others to know that we always speak the truth and that we can be trusted. God knows when we're truthful, and it makes him happy. It also makes others happy when they know they can trust us to be honest.** Ask:

★ **In what ways can being honest help others believe us?**

★ **How are truth and trust connected? Which comes first: honesty or trust? Explain.**

★ **Why is it important to be trustworthy and honest?**

★ **How can you be more honest in what you say and do?**

Say: **God is always honest and truthful. That's why we can trust him completely. And God wants us to follow his example. We can choose to** be truthful to God, to others, and to ourselves. God helps us be truthful by setting a perfect example of honesty. God helps us be truthful with his Word, too. Let's discover how learning God's Word helps us stay on the true path to honesty.

SUPER SCRIPTURE

Flip the lights several times, then turn them out as you ask kids to name things in the room. (If the room can be totally dark, so much the better!) After a few items are named, turn on the lights and ask:

★ **How do lights help us see more clearly?**

★ **How are dishonesty and lies like darkness?**

★ **In what ways is the truth like shining a bright light in darkness?**

★ **In what ways is God's Word like a light that helps us see more clearly?**

★ **How can we put the light of God's Word to work in our lives today?**

Say: **When we have light to shine on our path, we see truthfully what's there—whether it's rocky and bumpy or smooth. That's how God's Word helps us! Understanding Scripture and what God says gives light to our lives and helps us see truthfully where God wants us to be. God's Word is like a truth-filled light that shines on our path as we go through each and every day. It helps us steer clear of troubles and stay on the path that leads to him! Who can repeat Psalm 119:105, which begins "Your word is a lamp"?**

Let kids take turns repeating the verse, then repeat the verse two times in unison. If you have older kids who need an extra Scripture challenge, add in Psalm 119:104. Discuss how dishonesty is a "wrong path" and how, through learning and understanding God's Word, we can avoid that path with the truth.

Form pairs or trios and hand each child a paint stir stick. Explain that you'll be making Truth Batons to remind everyone how important it is to be truthful to God, others, and ourselves. Let children use markers to write the words to Psalm 119:105 on one side of the sticks. (If you prefer, make photocopies of the verse from page 126 and

Your word is a lamp to my feet and a light for my path.

glue it in place on the sticks. Also, have older kids write or glue the Scripture strip for Psalm 119:104 on the reverse sides of their stir sticks.) Then invite kids to tear lengths of crepe paper and tape them to the tops of the sticks as streamers. As you work, visit about why it's important to use God's Word in our lives and not just repeat the Bible's words.

When the Truth Batons are complete, say: **Honesty and truth are very important to trust, and trust is important in our relationship with God! A wonderful way to worship God and show that we love and respect him is through being truthful and honest. The Bible says we're to worship God in spirit and in truth. So let's worship God with a special prayer chant. We can use our Truth Batons to help!**

A POWERFUL PROMISE

Before class, make one photocopy of the Whiz Quiz on page 36 for each child.

Have kids remain in their pairs or trios and hold their Truth Batons. Say: **We've learned today that God is always truthful and honest and that by his example and his Word, we can be truthful to God, others, and ourselves. We know that truth starts in our hearts and comes out in our words and actions. And we've worked on the Mighty Memory Verse that teaches us how God's Word is a light that shines truth into our lives. Psalm 119:105 says,** (pause and encourage kids to repeat the verse with you—help older kids repeat verse 104 as well) **"Your word is a lamp to my feet and a light for my path."**

Hold up the Bible and say: **Because we know God is truthful, we trust him. And we can trust God's promises because God never lies—God does what he promises all the time! We can each commit to being truthful and honest in all we say and do this week. As we pass the Bible around the circle, we can make our own special promises. We can say, "I want to be truthful today and always, God."** Pass the Bible until everyone has had a chance to make a promise.

Say: **Now let's use our Truth Batons to worship God in spirit and in truth! As we repeat this prayer chant, tap your batons on the floor, together with your partner's batons, or in the air in time to the chant.** Begin by slowly repeating the following prayer, then repeating it two times more quickly. Encourage kids to tap in time to the syllables. End with a corporate "amen."

H-O-N-E-S-T—

Truth, truth and honesty!

God is truthful to you and me—

That's honestly how we should be!

Say: **As you go home today, remember that we're to be truthful to God, to others, and to ourselves. And smile, because truth starts in our hearts!**

Before kids leave, allow five or ten minutes to complete the Whiz Quiz from page 36. If you run out of time, be sure to do this page first thing next week. The Whiz Quiz is an invaluable tool that allows kids, teachers, and parents to see what kids have learned in the previous three weeks.

End with this responsive good-bye:

Leader: **May God's truth be with you.**

Children: **And also with you!**

Distribute the Power Page! take-home papers as kids are leaving. Thank children for coming and encourage them to keep their promises to God this week.

POWER PAGE!

So many good things happen when Jesus sets us free! Find and shade in the following words in the box. The letters left tell how we're set free.

✳ help   ✳ peace   ✳ serve
✳ honesty   ✳ power   ✳ trust
✳ love   ✳ safe   ✳ worship

W	O	R	S	H	I	P
H	O	N	E	S	T	Y
E	T	T	R	U	S	T
L	L	O	V	E	A	R
P	O	W	E	R	F	U
T	P	E	A	C	E	H

TRUE WISDOM!

WOW! Jesus sets us free with his truth! Discover what truth brings us from these wise sayings from Proverbs.

Proverbs 3:13, 14   Proverbs 14:25

Proverbs 12:19   Proverbs 16:13

Proverbs 12:22   Proverbs 19:8

Use the Word Bank to fill in the words to Psalm 119:105.

Word Bank Wonder

_____ _____ is a _____

___ my _____ ____ ___

_____ for ___ _____ .

lamp	a	feet	my
and	path	word	
to	your	light	

WHIZ QUIZ

Fill in the missing letters to recreate the key ideas from the lesson.

★ GOD'S WORD IS ◯◯◯Ⓔ.

★ GOD WANTS US TO BE ⒽⓄ◯◯◯Ⓣ.

★ WE CAN BE HONEST TO ◯◯Ⓓ, ◯ⓉⒽ◯◯Ⓢ, AND ◯ⓊⓈ◯◯Ⓥ◯.

★ JESUS IS THE Ⓣ◯Ⓥ◯◯.

★ WHO SETS US FREE? Ⓙ◯◯◯◯

★ GOD'S WORD IS IN THE ◯Ⓘ◯Ⓛ◯.

Color in any letters that appear in the circles above. What does the shaded letter stand for? →

K	M	A	F	C
T	B	O	E	H
M	A	G	C	A
Z	K	R	F	Y
X	W	N	C	Q
C	A	S	X	M
F	Q	U	K	A

is   my   word   feet

your

to

light

a

a

lamp

and

for

Psalm   path   119:105   my

← Draw arrows to place the words in their correct positions to complete the Mighty Memory Verse. The first word has been done for you.

LOVE & KINDNESS

Be imitators of God,
therefore, as dearly
loved children and
live a life of love.
Ephesians 5:1, 2

KINDNESS COUNTS

Jesus taught us to show loving-kindness.

John 13:4, 5, 12-15
1 John 4:19

SESSION SUPPLIES

★ Bibles
★ newspaper
★ small gifts such as erasers, wrapped candies, or pencils
★ tape, markers, and glue
★ margarine tub lids
★ scissors and paper punch
★ bowls of water
★ satin cord
★ soap and paper towels
★ photocopies of the "K-L-F 4 Jesus" circles (page 44)
★ photocopies of the Power Page! (page 45)

MIGHTY MEMORY VERSE

Be kind and compassionate to one another, forgiving each other, just as in Christ God forgave you. Ephesians 4:32

SESSION OBJECTIVES

During this session, children will
★ learn that God loved us first
★ understand that Jesus taught through example
★ discover that Jesus commands us to follow his example
★ explore ways to demonstrate loving-kindness

BIBLE BACKGROUND

Many lessons can be learned through reading, writing, and recitation, but the most thorough learning occurs through solid example and faithful imitation. Jesus provided us with perfect examples of love, kindness, and forgiveness in every step of his ministry. From healing the ten lepers to embracing the tough-to-love Zacchaeus to his ultimate example of love through dying on the cross to forgive our sins, Jesus modeled unconditional love and acceptance, kindness and caring.

In John 13, we discover how serving others was one way Jesus demonstrated his love. Jesus not only desired us to show loving-kindness to others, he specifically told us to follow his example in verse 15. Kids understand "follow the leader" and will immediately realize that we're to imitate

Jesus in loving, forgiving, and being kind to others, from those in their Sunday school class to family members, friends, and even foes.

POWER FOCUS

Before class, prepare the surprise paper cone by loosely rolling several sheets of newspaper into a cone shape and taping the seams. Slide tiny gifts such as small erasers, wrapped candies, or pencils inside one of the side pockets. During the presentation, you'll hold this secret pocket closed with your hand as you show the kids the "empty" cone. When you pull out the items, it will appear as if they've come from thin air! Practice holding and retrieving the goodies several times so your presentation is smooth.

Gather kids in a semi-circle and hold the paper cone with the hidden treats. Say: **The newspaper is filled with many sad pieces of news. But there are also stories of kindness and giving. What are stories about kind acts that you have heard from the newspaper, radio, or friends?** Invite kids to tell about kind things they've heard of, then ask:

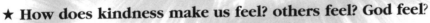

★ **How does kindness make us feel? others feel? God feel?**

★ **Why is it important to spread acts of kindness and love to others?**

Say: **The Bible tells us about so many times when Jesus was kind and loving. He healed the sick, was a friend to those who were hated, taught others kindly, forgave others with love, and even raised people from death! Jesus was and still is the perfect example of loving-kindness, and he's the example we want to follow.** Quickly show the inside of the newspaper cone. (Be sure to hold the pocket containing the gifts securely closed!) Then say: **Sometimes the news feels empty and filled with awful stories. We might wonder if there is any kindness or love left in the world. But when we love Jesus and follow the examples that he taught us, loving-kindness is alive and well and can be found in surprising places!**

Pull the small gifts from the newspaper and hand them out to children as you say: **When we give to others and do special things for them, we're** demonstrating kindness. And sometimes those gifts of love and kindness appear in surprising ways. Today, we'll learn about one surprising way Jesus showed love and kindness to others. We'll discover where love comes from and just how we can spread Jesus' loving-kindness to others we know—and even to those we don't know! And we'll begin learning a new Mighty Memory Verse about being K-L-F for Jesus! You'll find out more about those letters later! Right now, let's explore what the Bible tells us about Jesus' many acts of kindness, love, and forgiveness. Set the paper cone and the gifts to the side.

THE MIGHTY MESSAGE

Place a bowl of water, soap, and a paper towel on the floor. Look around at the children, then silently carry the water, soap, and towel and place them before one child. Without saying a word, wash the hands of that child and pat them dry with the paper towel. Then slide the water, soap, and towel aside. Ask:

POWER POINTERS

Kids of all ages struggle with being kind to bullies. Remind kids that Jesus wants us to love all people and that a little sugar sweetens even the sourest lemons!

★ What did I just do? Were you surprised? Why?

★ How did my washing someone's hands show kindness? caring? thoughtfulness?

Say: It might surprise you to know that washing people's hands is a kind way to serve them—especially if their hands need cleaning and they're unable to do it themselves. Jesus taught us about serving others as a way to demonstrate loving-kindness. Listen to how Jesus served his disciples on his last night on earth. Read aloud John 13:4, 5 and 12-15. Then ask:

★ In what way did Jesus serve his friends? show his love for them?

★ Why does Jesus want us to serve others and treat them kindly?

★ How did Jesus teach us by his example?

★ What did Jesus want us to do for others? Why?

Say: Jesus humbled himself to wash his disciples' dusty feet. He did this to show everyone—even presidents and kings—that we should treat others with loving-kindness. And serving others is one way to do this. Jesus teaches us to follow his example and serve others with love, kindness, and generosity. Ask:

★ Serving is one way to demonstrate love and kindness. What are other ways?

★ Who are people we can be kind to? whom we can serve?

Say: **Jesus wanted us to be kind to all people, not just to people we know. It's easy to love the people we know and like! The hard part is being kind, loving, and forgiving even to people we don't know or like. But Jesus teaches us by his example to be kind, loving, and forgiving to all people. Let's play a serving game to remind us that Jesus taught us to show loving-kindness to others.**

THE MESSAGE IN MOTION

Place newspapers on the floor at one end of the room about six feet apart. Set the bowls of water on the newspapers. Place soap and paper towels by the bowls. Have kids form pairs or trios. Explain that in this relay, partners must hop to the water bowls and wash and pat dry each other's hands. Then have partners hop back and give each other high fives. Tell everyone you'll allow three minutes for the race. At the end of three minutes, call time or flip the lights on and off. Ask:

★ **What did you and your partner do if someone else was at the bowl? Did you react with loving-kindness? Did you offer to help another pair? Explain.**

★ **How can acts of kindness and love change someone's view of the world?**

★ **In what ways does serving others and showing kindness draw us closer to God? to others?**

Say: **You know, serving isn't just something we do—it's something we give! That's just like love and kindness. When we have a kind heart and loving spirit, we naturally want to serve and help others. The Bible tells us that we love because God first loved us.** Read aloud 1 John 4:19. **Isn't that awesome?**

God invented love, and through Jesus we have perfect examples of how to show our love to others. God's Word tells us that God invented love, and it also tells us something about being kind to others. Let's learn a new Mighty Memory Verse about being K-L-F for Jesus!

SUPER SCRIPTURE

Before class, enlarge and photocopy the circle pattern on page 44. Enlarge the pattern so it will fit the plastic margarine tub lids when it is glued to them. Be sure you have a plastic lid and a circle for each child.

Have kids open their Bibles to Ephesians 4:32. Ask several volunteers to read the verse aloud, then ask what kids think the verse means. Say: **This verse tells us to be three things to others: kind, loving, and forgiving— or K-L-F, for the letters the words begin with. There's a big word in the verse: compassionate. Compassionate means loving. It means feeling what the other person feels and caring about those feelings. In this verse, we learn that we're to be kind, loving, and forgiving to one another, just as God is to us through Jesus. In other words, we can be K-L-F for Jesus! Ask kids to once again identify what the letters K, L, and F stand for in the verse.**

Hand each child a photocopy of the circle pattern and a margarine lid. Have kids color and cut out the circles, then glue them to the top of the lids to make colorful flying discs. Finally, punch holes in the lids so they can be worn as necklace medallions. (You'll add the cord later.) If you choose, photocopy the Scripture strip for Ephesians 4:32 (page 126) and glue it to the backs of the flying discs. As kids work, visit about ways to show loving-kindness to others, such as helping with chores, cheering up an ill or sad friend, or donating time to help an elderly neighbor.

When the flying discs are finished, form a large circle and take turns tossing the flying discs and repeating the Mighty Memory Verse in sections. Begin with "Be kind and compassionate to one another, forgiving each other," then "just as in Christ God forgave you." If you have young children in class, you may wish to use the word *loving* instead of *compassionate*. If you prefer, use only the first portion of the verse this week

After several minutes, say: **Sit in a circle and hold your flying discs. Think of how many times Jesus has loved, forgiven, and been kind to you. Now think of someone you can show loving-kindness or forgiveness to this week.** After several moments of silence, say: **Let's take a moment to offer a prayer of thanks for Jesus' perfect example of love and kindness and ask for his help in being more loving, kind, and forgiving to everyone.**

A POWERFUL PROMISE

Before class, cut the satin cord into one 18-inch length for each child.

Have kids form a circle, then say: **We've learned today that Jesus set the perfect example of loving-kindness by serving his disciples. We've read in the Bible that we love because God first loved us. And we've worked on the Mighty Memory Verse that says,** (pause and encourage children to repeat the verse with you) **"Be kind and compassionate to one another, forgiving each other, just as in Christ God forgave you."**

Hold up the Bible and say: **Let's make a commitment to be kind and loving just as Jesus has been to us. We can each commit to being K-L-F for Jesus and showing one act of kindness, one loving act, and one act of forgiveness this week. As we pass the Bible around our circle, we can make our own special promises. We can say, "I want to be K-L-F for Jesus every day."** Pass the Bible until everyone has had a turn to make her promise.

Hand each child a length of cord and say: **Let's join our circle by holding cords with the people you're standing beside.** Pause, then continue: **The Bible tells us that a strand of three cords cannot be easily broken. We can think of the way we all join together to show loving-kindness as a kind of loving cord that is strong and cannot be easily broken. If all of us show love and kindness to others, what a happier world we'll live in! Let's say a prayer thanking Jesus for teaching us how to be loving and how to serve others with kindness.**

After the prayer, have kids thread their cords through the holes in the flying discs and then knot the ends to make necklace medallions. Challenge kids to wear their medallions all day to encourage others to ask about the meaning of K-L-F 4 Jesus. End with this responsive good-bye:

Leader: **May Jesus' loving-kindness be with you.**

Children: **And also with you!**

Distribute the Power Page! take-home papers as kids are leaving. Thank children for coming and encourage them to keep their promises to God this week.

POWER PAGE!

FOUR Friendly Firsts!

1. Who loved us first?
   (1 John 4:19)

   _____

2. Who gave us the first Lord's
   Supper? (Luke 22:14-20)

   _____

3. Who was the first person to
   see Jesus after he was risen?
   (John 20:10-16)

   _____

4. What is the first and greatest
   commandment?
   (Matthew 22:37, 38)

   _____

Sweet Serving

Whip up a batch of sweetness to serve to
your friends and family! You'll need:

★ 1 box of vanilla wafers or graham
   crackers
★ 3 cups of strawberry yogurt
★ 1 container of whipped topping
★ 1 cup of frozen strawberries
★ cinnamon red-hots or red-hot hearts

Directions: Crunch the box of cookies and
place the crumbs in a 9-by-13-inch pan. In a
bowl, thoroughly mix the yogurt, whipped
topping, and frozen strawberries. Pour the
yogurt mixture over the cookie crumbs.
Scatter cinnamon candies on top, then
freeze your dessert for an hour or more
before serving. Mmm goood!

ONE OF A KIND!

Some of the words to Ephesians 4:32
are scrambled. Unscramble and write
them correctly in the boxes.

dnik　　　**gifnrovgni**　　　**nad**

thCisr　　　**ergofva**　　　**eno**

rohtnae　　　**tujs**

Now read down the shaded boxes to
discover what we're to give to others.

___ ___ ___ ___ ___ ___ ___ ___

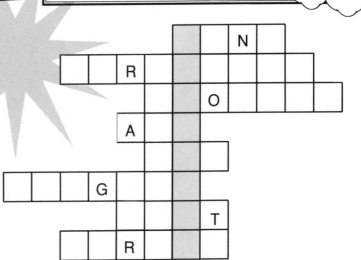

CARE-N-SHARE

Sharing blessings can change lives.

Luke 19:1-8
2 Corinthians 9:7

SESSION SUPPLIES

★ Bibles
★ cookies and icing
★ candy sprinkles
★ plastic knives and napkins
★ sandwich bags
★ rubber bands
★ newsprint, tape, and markers
★ photocopies of the paper doll on page 124
★ photocopies of Ephesians 4:32 (page 126)
★ photocopies of the Power Page! (page 53)

MIGHTY MEMORY VERSE

Be kind and compassionate to one another, forgiving each other, just as in Christ God forgave you.
Ephesians 4:32

(For older kids, add in Ephesians 5:1, 2a: "Be imitators of God, therefore, as dearly loved children and live a life of love.")

SESSION OBJECTIVES

During this session, children will
★ explore attitudes surrounding sharing
★ recognize that sharing can change lives
★ discover ways to share with others
★ learn that caring and sharing are ways to express love

BIBLE BACKGROUND

Think of the most loved "unlovable" Bible character you can imagine. Would it be Jacob? Saul? Or maybe Zacchaeus, the diminutive tax collector Jesus befriended with love, acceptance, and sharing? What seemed to be small acts of kindness on Jesus' part both surprised Zacchaeus and changed his life forever! Jesus spent his entire life modeling the kind of caring and sharing that draws people closer to God, lifts spirits in love and forgiveness, and changes lives in many joyous ways. We're told that God loves a cheerful giver, and whether we give and share of our time, talents, or money, we need to share freely and with a caring, happy heart as Jesus does for us. Isn't it appropriate, then, that the English word *hilarious* has its origins in the Greek word *hilaros,* which means "joyful, merry, gracious, and without grudging"?

Kids of all ages love the story of short-statured Zacchaeus and how his life was changed by sharing a meal with Jesus. It's important for children to understand that even the smallest acts of caring and sharing can have huge results. We may change a frown to a smile—or even a life of sin to a life of love in Jesus. Encourage kids to explore the values of caring and sharing the way God wants us to offer them—with cheerful hearts!

POWER focus

Before class, photocopy the paper doll pattern from page 124. Write the word "MOM" in bold letters at the top of the page. Practice folding and unfolding the paper according to the illustration. Fold the paper in half. Then fold the right half backward as you bring the left half forward. When you open the paper, the figure will be reversed so the word MOM spells the word WOW! (Kids will love this neat trick!) You'll be telling a short story as you fold and unfold the paper.

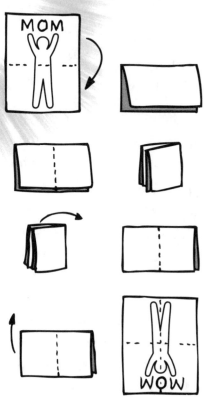

To begin, gather kids and place the paper beside you. Welcome children warmly and say: **I see a lot of happy faces here today! That's so nice to see. But I have a story to tell you about someone who didn't have a smile or happy attitude one day. Poor Anne woke up feeling grumpy and sad. It was just one of those days! She broke her shoelace, got toothpaste on her favorite sweater, then ran out of milk for her corn flakes. What a rotten day she was having!**

Hold up the picture that says MOM: **Anne's mom felt bad for Anne. She'd had plenty of sad and bad days, too! Have you ever felt like Anne?** Pause for kids to tell about their experiences, then continue: **At lunch time, Anne was still sad. Would she ever feel happy? And then she opened her lunch.**

Fold and unfold the page so the word WOW is showing and the doll is standing on its head. **Suddenly Anne's day went from ow to wow! Her mom had written a nice note and put it on a special cupcake just for Anne! Because Anne's mom had taken a moment to care and share in a special way, Anne's whole day got better right away!** Set the paper down, then ask:

★ How did caring and sharing change Anne's day? her mom's day?

★ In what ways can caring and sharing with others make us feel good? closer to God? closer to others?

★ Why do you think God wants us to care and share with others?

Say: **Anne didn't have much happiness that day, but Anne's mom did. So she shared her happiness with Anne—and look how it changed Anne's whole day! When we take time to care about others and share with them what we have, it can change their day and maybe even their lives! Today we'll be learning about sharing our blessings and ourselves with others. We'll also discover how caring and sharing are ways to demonstrate our love. Right now, let's explore one way Jesus shared his love and changed one grumpy guy's day—and life—forever!**

POWER POINTERS

If kids think they are too young to make a difference, assure them that nothing brings warmth and love like the smile and laughter of a child. It can be just the gift and lift that someone needs!

THE **MIGHTY** MESSAGE

Have kids stand in a circle, then say: **You can help me tell this Bible story. Whenever I say the word** *small* **squat down low, and whenever I say the word** *big* **stretch up tall. Our story comes from the book of Luke and is about a grumpy guy named Zacchaeus.**

Now Zacchaeus was a very *small* **man who collected taxes from people. No one cared for Zacchaeus because he took more money than he was supposed to and kept it for himself! Zacchaeus seemed like a** *big* **cheat, and his heart seemed very** *small.* **One day, Zacchaeus heard that Jesus was coming to town, so he climbed a** *big* **tree to take a peek. Zacchaeus had heard that Jesus cared for all people—even** *small* **people, but he wanted to see with his own** *big* **eyes. Zacchaeus crouched down** *small* **in the tree, but Jesus saw him**

and said, "Zacchaeus, come down. Let's go to your house to share a meal." Zacchaeus was surprised in a *big* way, but he scampered down from the tree. Zacchaeus and Jesus shared a *small* meal, and during dinner, Zacchaeus felt something strange and wonderful—he felt loved and accepted by Jesus! Because of Jesus' kindness and love, Zacchaeus changed in a *big, big* way! Zacchaeus gave back to the people all the money he had taken and even more. Zacchaeus's life had been changed forever—in no *small* way!

Have kids sit down, then ask:

★ **In what ways did Jesus change Zacchaeus's life?**

★ **How did Zacchaeus feel after Jesus shared a meal and cared for him?**

★ **Why did Jesus care for Zacchaeus and share with him?**

★ **In what ways did Jesus show his love to Zacchaeus?**

★ **What can we learn about sharing with others from Jesus' example?**

Say: **Jesus cared for and accepted Zacchaeus even when others wouldn't. Jesus even shared his time with Zacchaeus, and the tax collector's life was changed forever! Listen to what else the Bible tells us about caring for and sharing with others.** Read aloud 2 Corinthians 9:7. Then ask:

★ **How should we give to and share with others?**

★ **What are ways we can share with and give to others?**

Say: **God loves a cheerful giver. That means he wants us to happily and willingly give and share with and care for others. Just as Jesus changed Zacchaeus's life with his caring heart, we can change other people's days, attitudes, and even their lives when we take the time to care and share from all God gives us. What a difference we can make! Now let's make something else—a yummy treat to share with others to show we care!**

THE MESSAGE IN MOTION

Before class, photocopy the Scripture strip for Ephesians 4:32 from page 126. Photocopy two or three strips for each child. You'll also need to prepare a cookie treat for each child by decorating a prepared cookie and topping it with candy sprinkles. Place the cookies in sandwich bags, along with a Scripture strip. Then fasten the bags with rubber bands. Keep the treats for the kids secret until the Powerful Promise.

Set out the cookies, icing, plastic knives, candy sprinkles, sandwich bags, and napkins. (Any prepared cookies will work just fine!) Also set out the

49

Scripture strips and rubber bands. Explain that you'll be decorating special cookie treats to present to others.

Decorate the cookies and slide one cookie in each sandwich bag, along with a Scripture strip of Ephesians 4:32. Seal the bags with rubber bands. Have each child prepare one or two treat bags. As children work, visit about ways to show caring and sharing with others. Remind kids that even the smallest ways of sharing and the tiniest acts of caring can change someone's entire day!

When the tasty treats are complete, have your class present them to kids in another class or to the adults, if you've made enough treat bags. You may wish to make several dozen bags and take them to a local senior center or children's home for a caring community outreach. After the Care-n-Share cookie treats have been distributed, ask:

★ **How does it feel to share something you might wish you could keep?**

★ **In what ways is it good to put others first and share with them?**

★ **How do caring and sharing go along with being unselfish?**

Say: **It's so important to put others first and cheerfully share what we have with them. It's so important, in fact, that God put many verses in the Bible explaining how to share, when to care, and who we can show love and kindness to. Let's work on learning our Mighty Memory Verse and exploring what it means.**

SUPER SCRIPTURE

Write the words to the Scripture song on page 51 on a sheet of newsprint and tape it to a wall. Ask for several volunteers to repeat the Mighty Memory Verse (Ephesians 4:32), then remind kids that the big word "compassionate" means loving and caring. Review with kids last week's lesson, especially what the letters K-L-F mean. Remind children that the letters stand for values we want to develop in our lives: kindness, love, and forgiveness.

Say: **It's important to be able to repeat God's Word, but it's just as important to know what God's Word means. What do you think God meant in Ephesians 4:32?** (If you have older kids who need a challenge, add in Ephesians 5:1, 2a. Discuss what they think it means to be imitators of God and to live a life of love.)

After kids share their thoughts, say: **God wants us to be kind, loving, and forgiving. We learned last week that serving others was one way to do** this. Now we're discovering that caring for others and sharing with them are other ways to be kind, loving, and forgiving. Jesus gave us a wonderful example of sharing and caring when he accepted Zacchaeus, and we can follow Jesus' example. We can cheerfully share our time, our talents, our money or other donations, and even our love and joy about Jesus! And we can care for others by respecting, helping, and listening to them, which is exactly what God's Word tells us to do!

Teach kids the following song to the tune of "Ten Little Indians." Sing the song a few times until children are familiar with the words, then ask them where they've heard these words before. Explain that they have been singing Scripture, which is a great way to learn God's Word!

Be kind and loving to one another;
Be forgiving to each other,
Just as in Christ God forgave you—
Ephesians 4:32.

Sing the song once more as you invite kids to walk around the room shaking hands and giving each other gentle pats on the back or shoulder. Then say: **Being kind, compassionate, caring, loving, and generous with others does put a cheerful song in our hearts—and in God's heart, too! Now, let's use our hearts to offer a prayer and special promise to God.**

A POWERFUL PROMISE

Have kids sit in a circle, ask for a moment of silence, then say: **We've learned today that we can joyously care for and share with others in many wonderful ways. We discovered how Jesus shared his love with Zacchaeus and how it changed Zacchaeus's life forever. And we worked on the Mighty Memory Verse that says,** (pause and invite kids to repeat the verse with you) **"Be kind and compassionate to one another, forgiving each other, just as in Christ God forgave you" Ephesians 4:32.** (If you worked on Ephesians 5:1, 2a, repeat this verse as well.)

Hold up the Bible and say: **Caring and sharing with others can be even small acts of kindness, but they can change someone's day or life in very big ways. Let's make a commitment to look for ways to cheerfully care for and share with others this week. Think of someone whom you** could share with or care for in a special way. It may be a brother or a sister, a friend, a grandparent, or someone at school. It may even be someone who's hard to love as Zacchaeus was!** Pause for a moment, then continue. **As we pass the Bible around our circle, we can make our own special promises. As you receive the Bible, say that person's first name and "I want to be caring and more generous with you this week."**

Pass the Bible until everyone has had a chance to hold it. Then end with a prayer thanking Jesus for his loving examples of kindness that teach us so much and for his help in finding ways to care and share with others. End with a corporate "amen."

Hold up the treats you prepared earlier for the kids. Smile and say: **Now I want to share with you! Here's a yummy treat for you eat to remind you that cheerfully caring and sharing can change someone's day. I feel so happy to see your smiles that my day will be wonderful! Thanks for sharing you with me!** Hand out the treat bags.

End with this responsive good-bye:

Leader: **May God's caring love be with you.**

Children: **And also with you!**

Distribute the Power Page! take-home papers as kids are leaving. Thank children for coming and encourage them to keep their promises to God this week.

POWER PAGE!

Care-n-Share Calendar

Use a blank calendar or prepare sheets of paper to look like calendar pages. Divide each day into Care and Share columns. Jot down ways you showed caring and sharing to others. See how long you can keep a diary going of your kindness.

Monday, September 22

CARE	SHARE

CHEERFUL GIVER

If God loves a cheerful giver, just think how he will smile when you share with each person below! Write the way you can share or care for each person this week!

Family Member: I will ―――――
―――――――――――――――――――
―――――――――――――――――――

Special Friend: I will ―――――
―――――――――――――――――――
―――――――――――――――――――

God: I will ―――――――――――
―――――――――――――――――――

KINDNESS CODE

Use the code at the bottom of the box to supply the missing letters to Ephesians 4:32 and 5:1, 2a.

__ __ __ __ __ __ and __ __ __ __ __ __ __ __ __ __ __ __ to __ __ __
✓ ✖ ☛ ☉ ▼ ✳   ✤ ◆ ◗ ● ✰ ■ ■ ☉ ◆ ▼ ✰ ★ ✖   ◆ ▼ ✖

another, __ __ __ __ __ __ __ __ each other, __ __ __ as __ __ Christ
✤ ◆ ✛ ✰ ☉ ♥ ☉ ▼ ✰   ✏ ✝ ■ ★   ☉ ▼

__ __ __ forgave __ __ __ . Be __ __ __ __ __ __ __ __ of God, therefore,
✰ ◆ ✳   ↔ ◆ ✝   ☉ ◗ ☉ ★ ✰ ★ ◆ ✛ ■

__ __ dearly __ __ __ __ __ children __ __ __ live a __ __ __ __ __ of love.
✰ ■   ❑ ◆ ♥ ✖ ✳   ✰ ▼ ✳   ❑ ☉ ✤ ✖

A	B	C	D	E	F	G	I	J	K	L	M	N	O	P	R	S	T	U	V	Y
✰	✓	✤	✳	✖	✤	✰	☉	✏	☛	❑	◗	▼	◆	●	✛	■	★	✝	♥	↔

RESPECTFULLY YOURS

It's important to respect and value others.

Matthew 7:12; 25:34-36, 40

MIGHTY MEMORY VERSE

Be kind and compassionate to one another, forgiving each other, just as in Christ God forgave you. Ephesians 4:32

(For older kids, add in Ephesians 5:1, 2a: "Be imitators of God, therefore, as dearly loved children and live a life of love.")

SESSION SUPPLIES

★ Bibles
★ plastic coins
★ plenty of plastic jewels
★ tacky craft glue and scissors
★ markers and crayons
★ a paper bag or a bowl
★ photocopies of the Skit
  Situations from page 124
★ photocopies of the card
  from page 60
★ photocopies of the Whiz
  Quiz (page 62) and Power
  Page! (page 61)

SESSION OBJECTIVES

During this session, children will
★ explore the meaning of respect
★ discover that valuing others means valuing Jesus
★ realize that love means respecting and valuing people
★ learn ways to respect and value God and others

BIBLE BACKGROUND

Think of things that were considered of great value in biblical days. Abraham's wealth was based in huge flocks of goats and sheep. Solomon's wealth consisted of unimaginable mountains of silver, gold, and jewels. Wealth in biblical days was defined in physical riches and material possessions—that is, until a poor carpenter came along and taught us that true wealth isn't counted in a bank book or collected in crowns and costly rings. Jesus taught us that valuing God and others with love and respect is the highest form of wealth we can achieve and the greatest treasure we can strive for.

All too often today we look at newspapers and listen to news shows and wonder, "Where has respect gone? Why don't we value people any longer?" It's not that these values are dead—they've just been buried under self-centered lifestyles. But the tide can turn. When even the youngest children learn about respect and valuing other people and their property, they get along better with friends and draw nearer to God. Help your children put the Golden Rule into action with this lively lesson on respecting and valuing others and God.

POWER focus

Before class, hide a plastic coin for each child. If you can't find plastic coins, use shiny pennies or nickels instead—kids will love it!

Gather kids and ask them to tell about people or things they value and treasure greatly, such as their families, friends, bicycles, or other items. Then say: **There are some valuables in this room. You'll have to look to find them, but see if you can find something we might consider a valuable treasure. If you find more than one, help someone who hasn't found a treasure yet.**

Pause while kids search out and find the coins. Then have kids return to their places. Say: **That was a fun treasure hunt. Did each of you find a valuable treasure? I found many, many treasures to value, and I didn't even have to leave this spot! Can you see the other valuables I found?**

Pause as kids look around, then say: **Each one of you is a treasure, and I value and respect you greatly! You know, we often think that the only real valuables in the world are silver and gold and sparkly jewels. But today we'll learn about valuing other people and showing others love through respect.** Ask:

★ **Who is someone you value? Why?**

★ **How do you show that person respect?**

★ **Why do you think it's important to treat others with respect? to show that we value them?**

Say: **When we have kind and loving attitudes, we respect and value others. In fact, respecting and valuing others is a way to demonstrate our love. God loves and values us, and in return, we respect, value, and love him. Let's hear what the Bible says about how we're to treat others.**

Have kids put their coins away in a safe place.

THE MIGHTY MESSAGE

Have kids form pairs or trios, then say: **Our Bible passage today is found in the book of Matthew. Follow my actions as we act out this very important Bible passage and learn about how we're to treat and value others.**

Read or retell in your own words Matthew 25:34-36 and 40. Lead kids in actions described in the passage, such as feeding each other, giving each other something to drink, motioning them to "come in," pretending to help them dress, pretending to take their temperatures, and waving hello.

Then say: **That's an interesting Bible passage, isn't it? It says that when we love, respect, and value others, we're loving, respecting, and valuing Jesus, too. Wow! Just imagine—what if someone you met or a special friend were really Jesus in disguise? How would you treat him? What would you say? How would you behave?** Pause and invite kids to share their thoughts. Then ask:

★ **Why does Jesus want us to treat others with respect? to value them?**

★ **Who are we to respect and value?**

★ **How is the way we treat others a reflection of how we feel about Jesus? how we feel about ourselves?**

★ **In what ways are respect and valuing others a sign of the love in our hearts?**

Say: **When we respect people, we treat them with kindness and thoughtfulness. We aren't rude, and we don't put them down. When we value others, we're truly glad they're here with us on earth. We want them to know it, and we're willing to show it! What are ways to show others we respect and value them?**

POWER POINTERS

Kids often have problems with respecting other people and their property. Help kids understand that we want to treat others as though they were Jesus in disguise!

Encourage kids to share their ideas, which might include greeting others, being friendly and thoughtful, sharing with others about Jesus, and obeying God or other authority figures. Then ask children to identify how we treat older people, teachers, parents, and friends. Compare and contrast the different ways we show each group respect and value.

Say: **When we have a loving and thoughtful attitude, we can't help but be respectful because we're anxious to show others that we value them as people. We remember that we're to treat others as if they were Jesus in disguise! Let's use a few skits to help us demonstrate what it's like to respect and value others.**

THE MESSAGE IN MOTION

Before class, photocopy the Skit Situations from page 124. Cut the skit suggestions apart and place them in a bag or bowl for kids to draw out.

Form six groups and have each group draw out a skit situation, then brainstorm how they could react to the situation with respect. Give several minutes for groups to decide how they could act out the situation and response, then have each group perform its situation.

When each group has had a turn to act out a situation, ask:

★ **How can respect and showing we value people help us in dealing with others?**

★ **In what ways is respecting and valuing others a way of honoring God? of obeying God?**

★ **Would you like to be treated with respect and thoughtfulness? Why or why not?**

Say: **The Bible tells us to treat others in the way we want to be treated. Jesus said it best in Matthew 7:12.** Read aloud Matthew 7:12, then say: **This portion of Scripture is known as the Golden Rule. Why do you think that's a good name?**

Pause to let kids share their ideas, then say: **Jesus always treated people with respect, and he demonstrated his love for us in the way he valued our spirits and hearts. He valued us enough to die for our sins so we can live with God in heaven forever! We can follow Jesus' example by respecting and valuing others, too. And we can show God respect by valuing his Word! Let's review our Mighty Memory Verse as we learn more about demonstrating love and kindness to others through respect.**

SUPER SCRIPTURE

Before class, make photocopies of the card on page 60. Make two or three copies on stiff paper for each child.

Gather children and ask several volunteers to repeat the Mighty Memory Verse (Ephesians 4:32 for everyone; Ephesians 5:1, 2a for older kids). Ask kids why they think learning God's Word is a way to respect and honor God.

Review the letters K-L-F, which stand for kind, loving, and forgiving. Then sing the Scripture song from last week's lesson as a great way to review the Mighty Memory Verse.

Say: **Valuing God's Word is not only important, it can also be life-saving! When we know and understand what God's Word says, we can obey it. God wants us to be kind and compassionate to one another, and showing others we respect and value them is a good way to do that! Respecting and valuing God is every bit as important as respecting and valuing others. What are ways we can show God how much we respect and value him?** Lead kids to name ways, such as learning his Word, reading the Bible, obeying him, praying, and loving others.

Say: **Being kind, compassionate, and forgiving to one another shows our love. So does showing respect to and valuing people. Think of two or three people you could show your love to this week. We'll make those people appreciation cards to remind them that they're valued and to pass along God's Word as well.**

Hand each child two or three cards. Invite children to use markers and pretend jewels to decorate the cards. While children work, ask questions such as "How does showing others they're valued make them feel?" and "How can showing respect for someone change the way we feel toward that person?"

When the cards are complete, set them aside and say: **One way God expresses his love for us is through the loving promises he makes. And because God respects and values us, he always keeps those promises. Let's make a**

You really mean so much to me
More than any precious jewel—
For all you are I want to say,
"I think you're really cool!"

Be kind and compassionate to one another, forgiving each other, just as in Christ God forgave you.   Ephesians 4:32

promise of our own to God to show that we want to respect his command to be kind and compassionate to each other.

A **POWERFUL** PROMISE

Before class, be sure to photocopy the Whiz Quiz from page 62 for each child.

Have kids sit in a circle, ask for a moment of silence, then say: **We've learned today about respecting and valuing others and that these are good ways to express loving-kindness. We've explored different ways to show respect and discovered why valuing others is important and helpful in our relationships with them and with God. We've also worked on the Mighty Memory Verse.** Encourage children to repeat Ephesians 4:32 with you. (If you worked on Ephesians 5:1, 2a, repeat this verse as well.)

Hold up the Bible and say: **Let's make a promise to God to show we respect and honor him. Let's promise to show respect to everyone we meet this week and to tell at least two people how much we value them. As we pass the Bible around our circle, we can make our own special promises. We can say, "I'll treat others how I wish to be treated."** Pass the Bible until everyone has had a chance to hold it. Close with a prayer thanking God for his Word, which teaches us about respecting others and showing them that they're valued.

As kids hold their coins, say: **Let's close with a fun game. I'll count to three, then you flip your coin and catch it. If it lands heads, show someone respect by greeting that person and wishing him or her a great day. If you have tails, show someone you value him or her by saying something kind, such as "I value your smile" or "I value your helpful spirit."** Have children flip their coins three times, then say: **Take your coin home to remind you that even though we may value different things, we should all value and respect others just as Jesus did!**

Before kids leave, allow five or ten minutes to complete the Whiz Quiz from page 62. If you run out of time, be sure to complete this page first thing next week. The Whiz Quiz is an invaluable tool that allows kids, teachers, and parents to see what kids have learned in the previous three weeks.

End with this responsive good-bye:

Leader: **May God's caring love be with you.**

Children: **And also with you!**

Distribute the Power Page! take-home papers as kids are leaving. Remind kids to take their coins and appreciation cards home and to give the cards to the people they were designed for. Thank children for coming and encourage them to keep their promises to God this week.

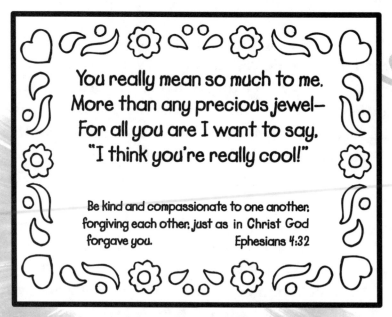

You really mean so much to me.
More than any precious jewel—
For all you are I want to say,
"I think you're really cool!"

Be kind and compassionate to one another,
forgiving each other, just as in Christ God
forgave you.   Ephesians 4:32

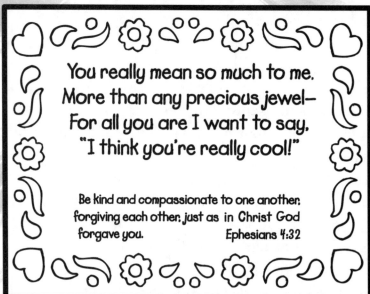

You really mean so much to me.
More than any precious jewel—
For all you are I want to say,
"I think you're really cool!"

Be kind and compassionate to one another,
forgiving each other, just as in Christ God
forgave you.   Ephesians 4:32

POWER PAGE!

NO DISGUISES!

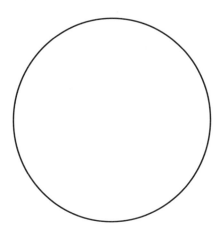

Draw a face wearing a funny disguise. Then think: If you met this person, how would you treat him? What would you say? Would you offer your help or friendship? Remember, we're to treat others as if they were

_____ in disguise!

(Matthew 25:40)

Remember the Rule

Read Matthew 7:12. This verse is known as the Golden Rule. Make a Golden Rule reminder to hang on your wall or give to a friend. Write the verse on a wooden ruler, then decorate it with gold glitter glue!

Do to others what you would have...

Valuable Verse

Make up a code to go with the missing letters in Ephesians 4:32. Then invite a friend to complete the puzzle and discover valuable Bible truth!

A	I	T
B	K	U
D	N	V
E	O	Y
F	R	
G	S	

__ __ __ __ __ __ and compassionate __ __ __ __ __ __

another, __ __ __ __ __ __ __ __ __ __ each other,

just __ __ in Christ __ __ __ __ forgave __ __ __ __ .

Ephesians 4:32

WHIZ QUIZ

Complete the sentences, then fill in the crossword.

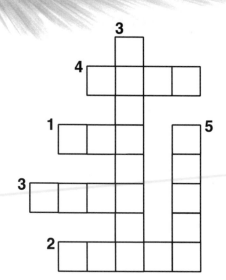

1. _____ loved us first.

2. _____ taught by example.

3. We can show K_____, L_____, and

    Forgiveness.

4. Zacchaeus changed his _____ .

5. Treat others as if they were _____ .

Follow the arrows to plug in the missing
letters to this puzzle from Ephesians 4:32.

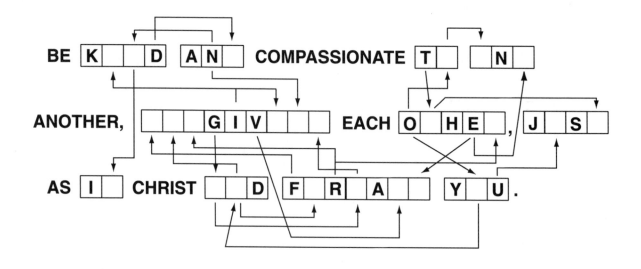

THANKFULNESS & PRAISE

I will praise God's name
in song and glorify
him with thanksgiving.
Psalm 69:30

GOD'S GREAT GRACE

God provides for our needs and wants.

Exodus 16:11-15
Philippians 4:19

SESSION SUPPLIES

★ Bibles
★ cardboard and a cereal box
★ tape and scissors
★ magazines and catalogs
★ ribbon
★ thin-sliced chicken
★ party bread
★ napkins
★ feathers and markers
★ tissue tubes or poster board
★ photocopies of Psalm 100:4 from page 126
★ photocopies of the Power Page! (page 71)

MIGHTY MEMORY VERSE

Enter his gates with thanksgiving and his courts with praise; give thanks to him and praise his name. Psalm 100:4

SESSION OBJECTIVES

During this session, children will
★ recognize the differences between needs and wants
★ discover that God provides for both needs and wants
★ explore the ways God provides for us
★ express thanks for God's provisions

BIBLE BACKGROUND

God's provision for his people is woven throughout the pages of the Bible in each story and every character's life. God's grace, abundance, and providing love were ever-present, sometimes discounted, often miraculous, but always faithful and faith-building—though not everyone recognized God's interventive provision or even thanked him for it. We encounter far more pleas for help than prayers of thanks offered to God. The Israelites had so much to honor, praise, and thank God for, including their freedom from slavery, safe escape from Egypt, and the food God sent to satiate their hunger. Yet the Israelites found words of unrest and complaint and failed to say the three most important words in response to God's provision: "Thank you, God."

What child hasn't forgotten to say thank you after receiving a special treat, help on homework, or a birthday gift? Words of thanks are often the most overlooked words in a child's (or adult's, for that matter) vocabulary. This lesson encourages kids to develop a lifestyle of thanksgiving and praise to God for all he provides in life, from laughter and love to truth and teaching. Help your kids recognize and respond to God's provision with thanksgiving, honor, and praise. Thank you, God!

POWER focus

Before class, use a large, empty cereal box and a piece of cardboard to prepare the Amazing Provisions box. Cut the cardboard to slide inside the box along one side to create a narrow hiding place. Tape the cardboard in place. The cereal box should appear empty when you look inside. (See illustration.) Then cut a 6-foot long piece of string or ribbon and tape magazine pictures of needs and wants to the ribbon. Pictures for needs could include nutritious foods, a house or other shelter, clothing, and water. Pictures of wants might include toys, bicycles, cake or ice cream, and a television set or stereo. Hide the ribbon in the secret opening in the box. When kids look in the box they will think that it's empty but be astounded when you pull out a long ribbon with pictures attached! Practice retrieving the ribbon from the box until you are smooth with the actions.

To begin, gather kids and hold the cereal box with the ribbon and pictures hidden inside. Ask children to tell about things they've always wanted or things they need. Then say: **This box of cereal provides for the need to feed our bodies. But look—it's empty!** Show kids the inside of the box. Hold the opening closed and gently shake the box to show that it's empty. Then say: **God provides for needs we may have, but unlike this cereal, God's provisions never run out!** Reach inside the cereal box and slowly pull out the ribbon with the pictures. Set the box aside.

Have kids unfasten the pictures and identify whether they think each represents a need or a want and place them in respective piles. Then ask:

★ **What's the difference between a need and a want?**

★ Do you think God provides for needs and wants equally? Explain.

★ In what ways does it help to know that God supplies what we need? much of what we want?

Say: **Needs and wants are different. Needs are things we need to live every day, such as nutritious food, warm shelter, clothing, and love. Wants, however, are things we would like to have but can really live without, such as toys, television, or pop and chips. God knows both our needs and our wants, and we can trust God to supply our needs. Sometimes God chooses to give us what we want as well! Today we'll be exploring how God provides for our needs and wants. We'll discover how we're to react to God's blessings. And we'll be learning a new Mighty Memory Verse to show God how much we need his Word. But now, let's find out how God made a miracle happen to provide for his people long, long ago!**

POWER POINTERS

Kids often wonder why God doesn't always give them what they want. Explain that God's choices for us don't always agree with our wishes, but we can trust God's choices to be the best!

THE **MIGHTY** MESSAGE

Hand each child a napkin as you say: **God provides for us in many ways—and sometimes those ways are real miracles! Our Bible message comes from the book of Exodus, and it tells about the time Moses and the Israelites were wandering in the wilderness after God had freed them from slavery in Egypt. You can help tell the story.**

Have kids form two groups and designate one group the quail and the other group the manna. Hand the quail kids each several pieces of thinly sliced chicken on napkins and explain that when they hear the word *quail* they're to give a piece of pretend quail to someone in the manna group. Give the manna kids each several slices of bread and explain that when you say the word *manna* they're to provide a piece of bread to someone in the quail group. Tell children you'll eat the quail and manna later.

Tell the following story of God sending the quail and manna from Exodus 16:11-15. Say: **God's people had been wandering in the wilderness for many days and were very hungry! They grumbled and mumbled. So**

Moses prayed and talked to God for the people. God heard Moses' prayers as well as the grumblings of his people, so he provided for their needs. God sent the Israelites *quail* to eat every evening.

Pause for kids to hand out the pretend quail, then say: **And in the morning, he sent sticky *manna* to munch.** Pause for the bread to be distributed. **The *quail* were plump little birds that tasted so good when roasted.** Pause. **And the *manna* was like bread from heaven that clung to the ground and bushes like sticky dew**. Pause. **God had provided for his people, but the people forgot something very important. They forgot to say thank you to God with happy hearts!**

Be sure each child has two pieces of bread and two slices of pretend quail. Have children make tiny sandwiches, then place the sandwiches on their napkins. Ask:

★ **Did God know what his people needed? Explain.**

★ **Why do you think God provided for Moses and the Israelites?**

★ **How was God's provision a demonstration of his love? caring? faithfulness?**

★ **What should God's people have done after receiving all God had given them? Why?**

★ **Did you thank whoever gave you bread or meat? Explain.**

★ **Why is thanking others important? Why is thanking God important?**

Say: **God knew what his people needed, and God provided for their needs. But the people forgot to thank him and continued to grumble. We have pretend quail and manna sandwiches. Let's show the Israelites how they could have thanked God by sharing a prayer thanking God for what he gives us.**

Pray: **Dear God, thank you for providing for our needs. We know your provision is a way you show your love for us. Please help us always be grateful. Amen.** Invite kids to nibble the sandwiches as you read aloud Philippians 4:19, then ask:

★ **What are ways God provides for you?**

★ **How do you thank God for what he gives you?**

Say: **God provides for what we need, and he often chooses to supply what we want as well. The Israelites needed nutritious food, and God gave that to them. Maybe they wanted cake and ice cream, but God chose to give them what was best to meet their needs. Sometimes we think we know what we need better than God, but God knows best! And our job is to thank him when he provides for us. Thank you, God! Now** let's have a bit of fun providing items to help each other make special birds of praise.

THE MESSAGE IN **MOTION**

Be sure you have an empty tissue tube for each child. (You can make stiff paper tubes by rolling 6-inch squares of poster board and taping the seams securely.) You will also need a Scripture strip of Psalm 100:4 (page 126) for each child.

Place the paper tubes, feathers, tape, and markers in separate piles in the center of the room. Form groups of four and have each group decide which member will be the tuber, which will be the feather-finder, which will be the taper, and which will be the marker runner. Explain that each person will make a pretend quail from the supplies and that certain people in the group will help provide the needed items.

Tubers will get the tubes each group needs. Feather-finders will supply each child with three feathers. The tapers will bring pieces of tape to the group members, and the marker runners will provide markers to decorate the pretend quail. Encourage kids to thank one another for their help and provisions. As children work, have them chat about ways God has provided for them and ways we can thank God for his provision.

When the birds are complete, have kids hold the feathery friends high for all to see. Then ask:

★ **How did it help to have someone provide for your needs in this activity?**

★ **How did you feel when you were thanked for what you provided?**

Say: **I can provide the last part of your quails. Let's tape our new Mighty Memory Verse to the quails to remind us to thank God for all that he gives.** Hand each child a Scripture strip to tape on the quail, then read the verse aloud. Say: **We know how nice it feels when people appreciate what we do for them. Just think how happy God is when we thank him for all that he gives us! We'll use our quails later to thank God for all he gives, but now let's fly our birds to the wall and let them rest and**

nest while we learn our new Mighty Memory Verse! Have kids set their birds aside.

SUPER SCRIPTURE

Place several sets of chairs throughout the room as if they're gates. Place a table or two in the room for the courts. Have kids open their Bibles to Psalm 100:4. Ask several volunteers to read aloud the first portion of the verse or have kids follow along silently as you read the first portion of the verse aloud three times: "Enter his gates with thanksgiving and his courts with praise." If you have older kids in class, repeat the entire verse.

Then say: **This verse is so special because it reminds us to come before God with thanksgiving and praise. That's something the early Israelites forgot to do—but we don't have to forget! We're to do two things: enter God's gates with thanksgiving, and enter his courts with praise. That means we come before God in two ways: with thanks and with praise.**

Let's play a fun game with these tables and chairs. When I say "Enter his gates," you walk between the chairs and say "thank you, God." And when I say "Enter his courts," scoot under the table and out the other side as you say a few words of praise, such as "You're powerful, God" or "You provide for us."

Play the game several times, then choose children to be the callers. After several minutes, ask kids to sit in a circle. Invite them to repeat the first portion of the verse twice. (Older kids can repeat the entire verse.) Then say: **When we take the time to really learn God's Word, it's a wonderful way to thank God for all that he gives us. Remember, God gave us his Word to help us and to teach us! We needed guidance and truthful teaching from God, and he provided it through his Word in the Bible. We can show God we're glad for his Word by learning and using it! And now we can use our feathery quails to thank God for his Word and for how he provides for our needs and wants every day.**

A POWERFUL PROMISE

Have kids hold their paper quail as they sit in a circle. Ask for a moment of silence, then quietly say: **We've learned today that God provides for our needs and often chooses to give us what we want. We know that God's**

provision is a way he shows us his love. And we've worked on the
Mighty Memory Verse, which tells us to come before God with thankful hearts. Psalm 100:4 says, (pause and encourage kids to repeat the
verse with you) **"Enter his gates with thanksgiving and his courts
with praise."** (Complete the entire verse with older kids.)

Hold up the Bible and say: **God promises to provide and care for
us through his love. And now, through our love, let's make a
promise of our own to God. We can each commit to expressing
our thanks to God every day this week. As we pass the Bible
around the circle, we can make our own special promises. We
can say, "I will give thanks to you, God."** Pass the Bible until everyone has had a chance to hold it.

Say: **Look at the feathers on your quail. As we go around the circle in
prayer, you can thank God for someone or something. We'll continue
going around the circle until we've said thank-you's for each feather
represented on our quails. Ready? I'll begin. Dear God, I thank you for
everyone in our class.** Continue around the circle until everyone has had a
chance to thank God the number of times that there are feathers on each
quail. Then end with a corporate "amen."

Say: **Take your quaily birds home and set or hang them in a place
where they'll remind you to give thanks to God for what he gives you
each day. If you really try, I know you can thank him as many times as
there are feathers on your quail!**

End with this responsive good-bye:

Leader: **May God's love be with you.**

Children: **And also with you!**

Distribute the Power Page! take-home papers as kids are leaving. Thank children for coming and encourage them to keep their promises to God this week.

POWER PAGE!

Needs or Wants?

Sometimes the things we think we *need* are just things that we *want*. To help you tell the difference, put an N beside Needs and a W beside Wants.

★ a ham sandwich ___
★ new toys ___
★ warm blankets ___
★ someone to love us ___
★ a television ___
★ tickets to the fair ___
★ the Bible ___
★ a red bicycle ___
★ God's Word ___

Now circle everything we're to thank God for.

MANNA CRUNCHIES

This is a heavenly good treat to share with a friend ... after you've given thanks to God!

You'll need:
❑ 3 cups of graham cracker cereal
❑ 1 jar of marshmallow creme
❑ 1 cup of shredded coconut
❑ butter or oleo

Mix everything in a buttered bowl—it will be sticky! Spread the mixture in a buttered pan and chill in a refrigerator for at least one hour. Cut into pieces and enjoy munching and crunching your tasty manna!

Fill-'em-In

Use Psalm 100:4 to fill in the missing words to the verse. Then fit the words in their correct places in the crossword.

_____ his _____ with _____
  1   2   3

and _____ _____ with _____;
     4   5   6

_____ thanks to _____ and praise
  7   8

_____ _____ .
  9   10

THREE LITTLE WORDS

God wants us to have a spirit of thankfulness.

Luke 17:11-19
Ephesians 5:19, 20

SESSION SUPPLIES

★ Bibles

★ newsprint and tape

★ markers and scissors

★ shoe boxes

★ rubber bands

★ wrapping paper

★ index cards and pencils

★ photocopies of Psalm 100:4 from page 126

★ photocopies of the Power Page! (page 79)

MIGHTY MEMORY VERSE

Enter his gates with thanksgiving and his courts with praise; give thanks to him and praise his name. Psalm 100:4
(For older kids, add in Psalm 100:5: "For the Lord is good and his love endures forever; his faithfulness continues through all generations.")

SESSION OBJECTIVES

During this session, children will

★ realize we need to live thankful lives

★ learn that we thank God for all things

★ understand the difference between praise and thanks

★ discover that learning Scripture is a way to thank God

BIBLE BACKGROUND

The lifestyles of the rich and famous weren't much different in biblical days than they are today. Solomon enjoyed a lavish lifestyle counting countless gems, jewels, and gold stored in his palaces. His father David experienced a life of adoration and power, while Nicodemus lived as a powerful religious leader in the midst of Jerusalem's social circles. But each of these lifestyles had one thing in common—they were all lived by people who thanked God in every circumstance, good or bad. In fact, the closer people lived to thanksgiving and praise, the nearer they lived to God!

One of the toughest lessons anyone can learn is being thankful to God in all things. "How can I thank God when

I'm ill?" "Why should I offer praise if God doesn't answer prayers the way I want?" Children especially have a difficult time understanding that thankful hearts and praise-filled lives don't depend on earthly circumstances or worldly possessions but on God's will and our faithful trust in a loving Father. Help kids learn that God wants us to live thankful lifestyles, ones that are filled with praise and honor for God. When kids choose and use those three little words—"Thank you, God"—they grow ever nearer to their loving Father!

POWER FOCUS

Warmly greet kids and thank them for coming. Then explain you'll start off your time together with a little game. Read the sentences below. Have kids jump and say "Thank you, God" if they think that it's a praise situation or quietly sit or kneel down if they think that it's not.

- ★ **The sun is shining on your picnic day.**
- ★ **You miss school because of a cold.**
- ★ **Your new bike has a flat tire.**
- ★ **The church finishes its new addition.**
- ★ **You're going to the zoo as you'd hoped.**
- ★ **Your friend lost her favorite pencil.**
- ★ **Dad made spaghetti for dinner.**
- ★ **Grandma is coming for a visit.**
- ★ **You lost a tooth.**
- ★ **You have spinach to eat for lunch.**

For extra fun, invite each child to name a new situation. Then have kids sit in a group and briefly discuss why not everyone thanked God or sat down for the same things. Ask children to tell why they thought some things were worthy of thanks and some were not. Then ask:

- ★ **Have you ever forgotten to thank someone for something they've done for you or given you? How did you feel afterward?**
- ★ **How does God feel when we give thanks? when we forget?**
- ★ **What things are we to give thanks for? Explain.**
- ★ **In what ways does giving thanks demonstrate our love for God? our appreciation? our faith?**

Say: **We all have different things we feel thankful for, but it might surprise you to know that God wants each of us to be thankful in all things! Today we're going to discover why it's important to give thanks** to God in all situations and to praise God continually. And we'll learn three little words that can change our lives and make God smile! Now let's listen to what the Bible tells us about being thankful through a story of how Jesus helped ten sick fellows who forgot to say the three simplest words in any language!

THE MIGHTY MESSAGE

Before class, write the following words and pronunciations for "thank you" on sheets of newsprint and tape them to the wall for kids to see: danke (DAWN-ka), merci (MARE-see), gracias (GRAW-see-us), asante (ah-SAWN-tay), and odeka (OH-de-ka). Each of these words says "thank you" in a foreign language. *Danke* is from German, *merci* from French, *gracias* from Spanish, *asante* from Swahili, and *odeka* from Hebrew, which is what the Israelites would have used to say thank you.

Gather kids in front of the newsprint and say: **There are many ways to say thank you, and each language has its own way. Let's see how they say thank you in a few different languages.** Have kids repeat each word with you a few times. Explain which language each word is from. Then say: **Three little words—"thank you, God"—have big importance no matter what the language they're said in! Let's hear how Jesus helped ten men who could have said these words, who should have said these words, but who didn't.**

Our Bible story is found in the book of Luke in the New Testament. One day, Jesus was walking along the road to Jerusalem. He was by the country of Samaria, where many people didn't know or love God. As Jesus came to a village, ten men with leprosy called to him. Now leprosy was a very bad skin disease, and these men wanted to be healed so much! **What do you think the men did?**

Pause for responses, then continue: **The men asked Jesus to help them. "Jesus, have pity on us!" they cried. And what do you think Jesus did?** Allow kids to tell their ideas. **Jesus told them to go to the priests. But as**

POWER POINTERS

It's important for kids to realize that we don't always understand God's ways or choices but that we can still trust God and thank him for his will and love in all situations.

the men were leaving, they were suddenly healed! What did the men do then? What would you have done?

Let kids share their thoughts, then say: **You'd think the men would have praised God. You'd think the men might have thanked God, but in the end, only one man came back to thank Jesus! He threw himself at Jesus' feet and thanked him. And guess who this man was? He was a Samaritan! No one expected this man to thank God for his help, yet he was the only one who took the time to express his love and thanks to God. Wow! What can we learn about thanking God from this man?** Pause for kids' responses.

Say: **God must have smiled at that man from Samaria. You know, God wants us to be thankful and to express our thanks for his loving-kindness and help. In fact, we want to live a thankful life in which we always remember to thank God first before we do anything else. But when do we thank God? And what do we thank him for? Let's see what the Bible says.** Ask a volunteer to read aloud Ephesians 5:19, 20. Then ask:

★ **Why is it wise to thank God for all things and in all situations?**

★ **Is it always easy to be thankful in everything? Explain.**

★ **How does a thankful spirit draw us near to God? help us love God more? help us have more faith?**

Say: **It isn't always easy to see the blessings in every situation, and it's not always easy to thank God for everything. But when we trust and love God, we can know that he will make even the hardest situations turn out the way he sees best. And our job is to be thankful in all things, even when it's hard. Ephesians 5:19 tells us to sing and make music in our hearts to the Lord, so let's make some music to God to express our thanks and praise. We can use our new words of thanks to help us!**

THE MESSAGE IN MOTION

Before class, collect a shoe box for each child. If you need to use other boxes, be sure rubber bands can fit across them and they have one open side. You'll also need one copy of the Scripture strip for Psalm 100:4 (page 126) for each child.

Hand each child a box and several rubber bands. Explain that in biblical times, many Israelites played lyres or harps to praise God. These instruments were like small, hand-held harps and stringed instruments. Tell kids that they'll be making crisscross harps to help praise and thank God with music.

Have kids use tape and festive wrapping paper to cover three sides of their boxes. Direct kids to tape a Scripture strip for Psalm 100:4 somewhere on their boxes. Then show kids how to attach the rubber bands lengthwise and crosswise on their boxes. When the strings are plucked, they'll make various tonal sounds. Point out how the shorter cross bands make lower sounds than the more stretched rubber bands. You may wish to have kids write the words for "thank you" in the different languages on the boxes.

As kids work, explain that David often played a small harp to thank and praise God. Tell kids they can read the words to many of David's songs and poems in the book of Psalms. Point out that Psalm 100:4, the Mighty Memory Verse, was written to thank God for his love and power.

When the crisscross harps are complete, use them to sing the following song to the tune of "Old MacDonald." Sing in front of the newsprint words until kids are familiar with the ways to say thank you in different languages. Then invite kids to strum, tap, and drum on their harps as they sing the song through one more time.

**God we sing our praise to you;
Thanks for all you do!
In every way you help us, Lord;
We sing our thanks to you!
Asante here, *merci* there;
Danke, odeka everywhere—
God we sing our praise to you;
Thanks for all you do!**

Say: **That was wonderful! I know God must be smiling. Just think of how nice it feels to be thanked and appreciated. And all it takes is three little words: Thank you, God. When we live a life of thankfulness, we can't help feeling happy, helpful, and full of smiles. No wonder God wants us to be thankful in everything!** Ask:

★ **What can you thank God for today?**

★ **How can you express your thanks?**

Say: **We've learned that we can thank God in many languages and with different words. We've also expressed our thanks to God through a special song. Now let's show God we thank him for his Word by working on our Mighty Memory Verse.** Have kids set their crisscross harps away until later.

SUPER SCRIPTURE

Have kids repeat the Mighty Memory Verse from last week (Psalm 100:4) three times. (Older kids repeated the entire verse last week, but younger children only worked on the first portion, so add in the remainder of the verse if needed, and be sure to repeat it three times.)

Then say: **This important verse tells two places to go and two things to do for God. It tells us to enter God's gates and to enter his courts, and it tells us to thank God and to praise his name. Listen to the patterns: gates with thanksgiving, courts with praise; to thank him, to praise him. Picture for a moment going through God's gates to thank him, then going through God's courts to praise his name. That makes a nice picture in our hearts and minds! Again, we're told to go two places to do two things.**

Have kids tell where we're to go and what we're to do. Then repeat the verse in unison two more times. If you have older kids, add Psalm 100:5 and point out that this verse tells three reasons to thank God: because he is good, for his love, and for his faithfulness. Also point out that the words *endures, forever,* and *continues* are all similar, showing that God is eternally worthy of thanks and praise! Have older kids repeat this verse three times aloud.

Ask kids to explain what the differences between thanking God and praising God might be. Then hand each child two index cards and a pencil. Say: **We praise God for who he is: for being powerful and mighty, loving and faithful. And we thank God for what he does, such as helping us, giving us his Word, or loving us no matter what. One of your cards is a thanking card and one is a praising card. Write or draw a thank-you to God on the thanking card. Then, on the praising card, write a word that praises God, such as powerful, loving, truthful, or faithful. When you're done, take a moment to decorate your card if you wish.** Encourage kids to work in pairs or trios and to help each other with words and ideas. Help young children write their words of praise.

When the cards are complete, say: **Learning and understanding God's Word is a wonderful way to thank and praise God, isn't it? And because we have so many things to be thankful for, we want many ways to show our thanks. We can offer a promise and prayer thanking God for his faithful love. We'll use our word cards to help.**

A POWERFUL PROMISE

Have kids hold their cards and sit in a circle. Ask for a moment of silence, then say: **We learned today that we're to live thankful lives and thank God in everything even if it's hard. We also discovered that there's a difference between thanking and praising God and have even explored a few ways to express our thanks and praise in different languages. And we worked on the Mighty Memory Verse that says,** (pause and encourage kids to repeat the verse with you).

Then hold up the Bible and say: **The Bible tells us that God's love and goodness endure forever—just like his promises. So let's honor God with a promise to be thankful in everything for the entire week—even when it's hard! As we pass the Bible around the circle, we can make our own special promises. We can say, "In everything, I will thank you, God."** Pass the Bible until everyone has had a chance to hold it.

Have kids form a standing circle. Say: **Let's quietly and reverently enter God's gates with thanksgiving and his courts with praise. We'll take a few steps toward the center of the circle and one by one read our thanksgiving cards aloud. Then we'll step backward and read our praise cards. Listen with a happy, thankful heart as each card is read, thanking God in your heart with all your love.** When all the cards have been read, end with a corporate "amen."

Close with this responsive good-bye:

Leader: **May a thankful heart dwell in you.**

Children: **And also in you!**

Distribute the Power Page! take-home papers as kids are leaving. Remind kids to take home their crisscross harps. Thank children for coming and encourage them to keep their promises to God this week.

POWER PAGE!

List Your Thanks

List things to thank God for that begin with each letter in the word thanks.

T _____

H _____

A _____

N _____

K _____

S _____

Number Thanks

Follow the example to solve the problems, fill in the letters from the key, then transfer the letters to the blanks below. 10 lepers, 1 gave thanks, so how many forgot? __9__

6 - 2 + 1 = ____

3 + 3 + 4 = ____

2 - 2 + 6 = ____

5 - 2 - 1 = ____

2 + 2 + 0 = ____

10 - 2 + 1 - 1 = ____

1 + 6 - 7 = ____

7 - 2 - 2 = ____

7 + 4 + 2 = ____

8 + 1 + 3 = ____

KEY	
0 = H	7 = L
1 = F	8 = N
2 = G	9 = V
3 = I	10 = A
4 = E	11 = O
5 = T	12 = R
6 = S	13 = K

What do we give thanks for?

__ __ V __   __ __ __ __ __ __   __ __ __
2 3 9 4   5 0 10 8 13 6   1 11 12

__ __ __   __ __ __ __ __ __!
10 7 7   5 0 3 8 2 6

ALL MIXED UP!

WORD BANK

estag   mih   maen
reten   soutrc   vegi
ghaktinsnvig   eprisa

Unscramble the words in the word bank and put them in the spaces to write out Psalm 100:4.

_ _ _ _ _ _ his _ _ _ _ _ _

with _ _ _ _ _ _ _ _ _ _ _

and his _ _ _ _ _ _ _ with praise;

_ _ _ _ thanks to _ _ _ and

_ _ _ _ _ _ _ his _ _ _ _ _.

Psalm 100:4

THOUSANDS OF THANKS!

Let's express thanks to God in all we do.

Psalms 69:30; 148

SESSION SUPPLIES

★ Bibles
★ scissors and tape
★ twine and crepe paper
★ balloons
★ markers
★ drawing paper
★ praise music (CD or tape)
★ photocopies of the Praise Carols (page 86)
★ photocopies of the Whiz Quiz (page 88) and the Power Page! (page 87)

MIGHTY MEMORY VERSE

Enter his gates with thanksgiving and his courts with praise; give thanks to him and praise his name. Psalm 100:4 *(For older kids, add in Psalm 100:5: "For the Lord is good and his love endures forever; his faithfulness continues through all generations.")*

SESSION OBJECTIVES

During this session, children will
★ understand that God wants us to thank him
★ explore various ways to thank and praise God
★ express thanks to God and others in their lives
★ discover how love and thanksgiving are related

BIBLE BACKGROUND

God is the God of multiples. He blesses and forgives us in abundance. He chooses and uses us in a multitude of plans. God helps us and heals us, teaches and tests us in countless ways throughout our days. David recognized the multifaceted nature of our loving Father and strove to thank and praise him in just as many countless and varied ways. From the strumming of the harp strings to his own songs and dancing to poems, psalms, and more, David lived his life in thanksgiving and praise for all God is and for all God does.

God is a God of multiples, so why shouldn't we thank and praise him in just as many ways as David? Most children have an exuberant abundance of energy and expression that can be directed toward powerful praise to our loving Lord. During the previous two weeks, kids have been exploring all that thanksgiving and praise entail and why it's important to express our gratitude and love to God. Turn kids loose with this joyous celebration of thanksgiving and praise as you allow them to express their natural love for God with delightful ways to praise!

POWER FOCUS

Place scissors, twine, and several chairs at one end of the room, then have kids form as many groups as there are chairs. Explain that you'll allow a few minutes to devise unique ways to transport the chairs to the opposite end of the room. Point out that groups can use twine or muscle power or any other way to get their chairs moving. After a few minutes, have groups take turns moving their chairs to the other end of the room. Clap after each group displays its unique moving plan. Then gather the groups and ask:

★ **How did your group decide which way to move your chair?**

★ **Why were there so many different methods of chair moving?**

★ **Was any one group more successful than another in reaching the goal? Explain.**

★ **How is this activity like the different ways we choose to thank and praise God?**

★ **Is any one way best? Why or why not?**

★ **Which is more important: the method or the result? Explain.**

Say: **There are many ways to do even the simplest of things. And just as there are many ways to move chairs, there are many ways to thank and praise God. No one way is better than another. In fact, it's not so much the way we choose to say thanks as the result of our thanksgiving! When we honor God with praise and thanks, God smiles and knows we love him! Today we'll be learning different ways to tell God thank you. And we'll discover how love and thanks go together in our hearts and lives. But first, let's learn how David expressed his love for God and praised God in a beautiful poem found in the Bible.**

THE MIGHTY MESSAGE

Say: **David loved God and knew that God had done so many things for him. So David wanted to thank and praise God in a special way. In fact,**

David wanted all the earth to praise God! How did David choose to thank God? Through writing beautiful songs that we call psalms. Listen to a verse in one Psalm that speaks about thanking God.

Read aloud Psalm 69:30, then say: **Isn't that beautiful? Now let's read another beautiful Psalm. Turn to the book of Psalms in your Bibles. Remember, you can open your Bibles in the middle and find Psalms.** Pause. **Now find Psalm 148.** Help kids locate Psalm 148, then invite children to read silently as you read the Psalm aloud. Challenge kids to listen for who is to praise the Lord. When the reading is done, ask:

★ **Who is to praise the Lord?**

★ **How do you think this expression of thanks and praise made God feel?**

★ **How can we use words and poems to thank God? to praise God? to express our love to God?**

Say: **This Psalm calls for all the heavens to praise God. It also calls for all the earth to give praise to God. Let's form heaven and earth groups and praise God by illustrating this beautiful Psalm!**

Have kids form two groups: the heavens and the earth. Give each group paper and markers. In the heavens group, have pairs or trios of kids illustrate the angels praising God; the sun, moon, and stars; and clouds. Have pairs or trios in the earth group illustrate sea creatures, a storm with lightning, mountains and trees, animals, and people. Allow several minutes for kids to complete their drawings. Finish the pictures by writing captions such as "Angels praise God" and "The mountains praise God."

When the drawings are finished, read Psalm 148 aloud once more and have each group hold up its picture at the appropriate time. Then ask:

★ **How can pictures be a way to praise and thank the Lord?**

★ **Why is it important to give thanks to and praise God?**

Say: **Your praise pictures are lovely, and we'll use them in another way to praise God in a moment. Remember that we thank God for what**

POWER POINTERS

Help kids understand that the word thanksgiving is a compound word combining the words giving and thanks. Point out that the word instructs us what to do— not just what to feel!

he does and praise him for who he is. Doesn't it feel good to tell God we love him through our thanks and praise? It makes me feel like it could be a happy holiday! At Christmas, we deck the halls to show how glad we are for Jesus' birth. We can deck the halls right now to express how glad we are for God's love.

THE MESSAGE IN MOTION

Before class, photocopy the Praise Carols from page 86 for each child. You'll also need to choose a hallway to decorate. A hall in the children's area is ideal. Your kids will decorate the hall with festive crepe paper, bright balloons, and posters and then sing praise carols when classes let out.

Have kids stay in their pairs or trios and assign different decking details, such as crepe-paper hangers, balloon brigade, and picture-posters to hang the pictures made during The Mighty Message. Help the crepe-paper hangers twist and turn colorful crepe paper into long garlands to hang and drape in a hall-way. Play praise music as kids work on their labor of love.

When the hallway is decorated, hand each child a Praise Carols handout and help them fold the papers in half with the songs facing out. Then fold the papers in half again to make songbooks. Invite kids to decorate their books as you play music. Practice singing "We Sing Praise," "We Thank You, Lord," and "Strong & Powerful" to the suggested tunes.

Say: **God loves to hear us praise and thank him! And at the end of the day, we'll be singing our praise carols in the hallway to remind everyone to thank and praise God for all his loving care. But first, let's learn a song based on our Mighty Memory Verse.**

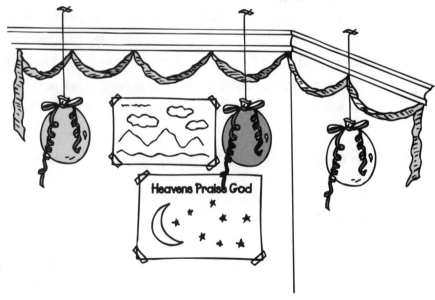

Heavens Praise God

SUPER SCRIPTURE

Repeat the Mighty Memory Verse (Psalm 100:4, plus 100:5 for older kids) aloud three times. Review the two places we're to go and the two things we're to do. With older kids, review the three reasons we're to do these things from verse 5.

Then say: **Learning and understanding God's Word is so important, but so is knowing how to use God's Word in our lives. Psalm 100:4 and 5 instruct us to come before God with thanks and to praise him, for God is good and his love will continue forever. How can knowing these truths help in our lives?** Allow children to share their thoughts, then ask:

★ **How are thanking and praising God ways to express our love?**

★ **In what ways can you thank and praise God every day?**

Say: **There are many ways to thank and praise God: from poems and songs to reading the Bible and telling others about God's love. And do you know the best part? When we express our thanks and praise, we're also expressing our love to God! One of our Praise Carols is sung to the tune of "Deck the Halls," but the words are based on Psalm 100:4 and 5. Let's practice that song right now and sing it with a heart full of thanks to our loving Father.**

Sing "Enter His Gates" on the Praise Carols handout to the tune of "Deck the Halls." Sing the song through several times, then say: **When we lift our voices to God, all of heaven smiles! God promises to care for us and help us, and in return, our natural response should be to thank and praise him for his love. Let's make a special promise to look for ways to express our gratitude to God for all he does in our lives.**

A POWERFUL PROMISE

Before class, be sure you've made a photocopy of the Whiz Quiz from page 88 for each child.

Have kids sit in a circle and ask for a moment of silence, then say: **We've learned today that expressing thanks and praise can be done in many ways and that all are wonderful. We've discovered that when we tell God thank you, we're also saying, "I love you." Finally, we've sung the Mighty Memory Verse that says,** (pause and encourage kids to repeat the verse with you).

Hold up the Bible and say: **Let's make a promise to God that we will always express our love, thanks, and praise for him—each day of our lives. As we pass the Bible around the circle, we can make our own special promises. We can say, "I will thank you forever, God, and praise your name."** Pass the Bible until everyone has had a chance to hold it.

Say: **In a moment, we'll go into the hall and sing songs from our Praise Carols songbooks, but right now, let's review all that we've learned in the past three weeks as we've learned about giving thanks and praise.** Allow five or ten minutes for kids to complete the Whiz Quiz from page 88.

Then go into the hall by your decorations and lead kids in singing the praise songs from their Praise Carols songbooks. Remind everyone passing by that we're to honor God with our thanks and praises every day! Then end with this responsive good-bye:

Leader: **May God's blessings be with you.**

Children: **And also with you!**

Distribute the Power Page! take-home papers as kids are leaving. Thank children for coming and encourage them to keep their promises to God this week.

PRAISE CAROLS

WE SING PRAISE

(Sung to the tune of "Old MacDonald")

God, we sing our praise to you;
Thanks for all you do!
In every way you help us, Lord;
We sing our thanks to you!
Asante here, merci there;
Danke, odeka everywhere.
God, we sing our praise to you;
Thanks for all you do!

WE THANK YOU, LORD

(Sung to the tune of "O, Tannenbaum")

We thank you, Lord, for all you bring.
Your blessings make us want to sing!
You love us so, and we hope you know
Our love for you will always grow!
Your power is an awesome thing.
You have control of everything.
We thank you, Lord, for all you bring.
Your blessings make us want to sing!

STRONG & POWERFUL

(Sung to the tune of "Jesus Loves Me")

You are strong and powerful,
Awesome Lord and wonderful.
We will sing our praise to you;
That is all we want to do.
We give you praise;
We give you praise;
We give you praise;
Our voices to you raise!

ENTER HIS GATES

(Sung to the tune of "Deck the Halls")

Enter his gates with thanksgiving—
Falalalala, la-la-la-la!
And his courts with praise we'll sing—
Falalalala, la-la-la-la!
Give thanks to him and praise his name—
Falala-lalala-la-la-la!
For he is good, and his love's the same—
Falalalala, la-la-la-la!

POWER PAGE!

Write Your Own Psalm

Praise and thank God by filling in your own words. Then read your psalm aloud to God!

O Lord, you are _____ ! You

give us _____ and _____ . Even

the _____ and _____

praise your name. You bring joy when

you _____ . You bring love

when you _____ . Forever I

will praise your _____ name!

THAT'S SOME PSALM!

Read the following Psalms, one each day for the entire week. You'll soon be singing psalms of praise.

Psalm 147   Psalm 100

Psalm 93   Psalm 148

Psalm 98   Psalm 23

Psalm 113

High & LOW

Use Psalm 100:4, 5 to fill in the missing high and low letters.

Enter his ⬜⬜⬜ with ⬜⬜⬜⬜⬜⬜⬜ and his

⬜⬜⬜⬜⬜ with praise; ⬜⬜⬜⬜ thanks to him ⬜⬜ praise

his ⬜⬜⬜. For the ⬜⬜⬜ is ⬜⬜⬜ and his ⬜⬜⬜

endures ⬜⬜⬜⬜⬜⬜ ; ⬜⬜⬜ faithfulness ⬜⬜⬜⬜⬜

through ⬜⬜⬜ ⬜⬜⬜⬜⬜⬜⬜ .

WHIZ QUIZ

Use the words in the word bank to complete the sentences, then transfer the numbered letters to fill in the blanks below.

✷ God sent _ _ _ _ _ to feed his people.
4   2

✷ Our _ _ _ _ _ _ _ gives us what we need.
8   1   5

✷ When we _ _ _ _ _ God, it shows our _ _ _ _ .
3   7

✷ The lepers should have thanked _ _ _ _ _ _ .
6

Father thank
Jesus manna
love

Write the letters in the blanks to discover how we're to be.

__ __ __ __ __ __ __ __
1   5   4   2   3   8   6   7

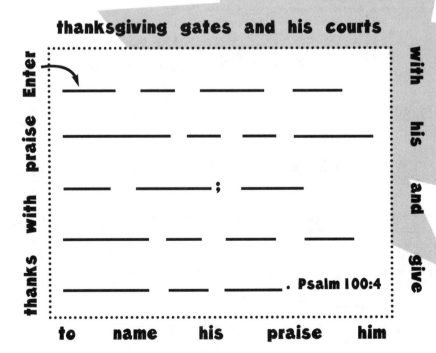

Draw arrows to place the words in their correct positions to complete the Mighty Memory Verse. The first word has been done for you.

thanksgiving gates and his courts

Enter praise

with his and give

thanks with

_____ ___ ___ ___

_____ ___ ___ ___ ___

___ ___ ___ ; ___

_____ ___ ___ ___ ___

_____ ___ ___ ___ . Psalm 100:4

to   name   his   praise   him

FORGIVENESS
& CHANGE

Forgive, and you will
be forgiven.
Luke 6:37

I'M SORRY!

If we forgive others, then we'll be forgiven.

Matthew 6:12, 14, 15; 7:12

SESSION SUPPLIES

★ Bibles
★ a copy of the boomerang pattern from page 125
★ poster board
★ markers and scissors
★ dominoes
★ treats (candies or pencils)
★ photocopies of the Power Page! (page 97)

MIGHTY MEMORY VERSE

Do not judge, and you will not be judged. Do not condemn, and you will not be condemned. Forgive, and you will be forgiven. Luke 6:37

SESSION OBJECTIVES

During this session, children will
★ realize the value of apologizing
★ discover that saying "I'm sorry" brings us nearer to God
★ learn that forgiving others leads to forgiveness for us
★ understand that Jesus commands us to be forgiving

BIBLE BACKGROUND

If we were to isolate the two most significant and life-altering cords consistently woven throughout the Bible, they would certainly be forgiveness and salvation. Forgiveness took various forms, from God's forgiving banishment from the garden to Christ's death on the cross. But though each man and woman in the Bible needed forgiveness, few actually offered it freely to others—and even fewer actively sought forgiveness from God. Perhaps it's our all-too-human egos that make forgiveness hard to seek and freely offer. Whatever the reason, Jesus came to teach us a different way to forgive. Put in simple terms, Jesus taught that whatever goes around comes around.

Even very young children understand the nature of "doing something wrong" and "punishment." And though they experience being forgiven for their mistakes, they often find it difficult to sincerely forgive others. Children need to learn that forgiveness is not only crucial in building strong, healthy, positive friendships and relationships with others but is also commanded by Jesus. Encourage your kids to explore their need to forgive as well as to ask for forgiveness in this lesson, which focuses on the Golden Rule and forgiveness through grace.

POWER focus

Before class photocopy and enlarge the boomerang pattern on page 125 and make several poster-board boomerangs to use as tracing patterns. Using markers, decorate one of the boomerangs to use in this activity.

To begin, have kids stand in a large circle and toss the boomerang to someone across the circle, then have that person toss it back to you. Continue until each child has had at least one turn to catch and return the boomerang. You'll probably need to move to the opposite side of the circle for some tosses. Then have everyone sit in place and ask:

★ **What do you call this bent little gizmo?**

★ **What are boomerangs famous for?**

★ **In what ways is a boomerang's returning action like how we treat other people?**

★ **Knowing this, how do we want to treat others?**

Say: **Real boomerangs can be fun to play with because they come back around. But so does the way we treat others. If we treat others with meanness, we'll probably be treated meanly, too. When we treat someone with kindness, we're treated kindly. And when we forgive others, we're forgiven in return. Today we'll be learning about forgiveness and how we can be forgiven for the wrong things we say and do. We'll discover who gave us the Golden Rule and why it's important to say "I'm sorry." And we'll also begin learning a new Mighty Memory Verse. But first, let's make special boomerangs to use during our lesson.**

Invite kids to trace boomerang patterns on poster board, then cut them out and decorate them with markers. As kids work, discuss times they offered someone forgiveness or times they've said "I'm sorry." Encourage kids to tell how they felt during their experiences. Make sure kids write their names on the boomerangs.

91

When the boomerangs are finished, say: **We'll fly our boomerangs over to the corner for awhile, then listen to some important advice Jesus gave us. Invite kids to toss the boomerangs aside until later.**

THE **MIGHTY** MESSAGE

Gather kids and ask:

★ **Why do you think it's important to apologize? to forgive others?**

★ **How can treating others with kindness and forgiveness help us cut down on apologies to others?**

★ **Which is easier: apologizing to someone or forgiving someone who apologizes to you? Explain.**

Say: **Apologizing means saying we're sorry for what we said or did that might have hurt someone else. And forgiving means accepting a sincere apology from someone and forgetting about the incident. Jesus had some strong things to say about the way we treat others and about forgiving. Let's hear what Jesus said from the book of Matthew.** Read aloud Matthew 6:12, 14, and 15. Then ask:

★ **What did Jesus mean in these verses?**

★ **Why is that sound advice?**

★ **What happens when we're forgiving? when we're not forgiving?**

Say: **God treats us fairly, and he wants us to know that when we don't forgive others, then we won't be forgiven either. But when we do show compassion and forgiveness, we'll also be shown forgiveness. That seems very logical and fair, doesn't it? Just like our boomerangs, what goes around comes around! And we want to be sure we're treating others with kindness and forgiveness right from the start! Listen to what else Jesus teaches us.**

Read aloud Matthew 7:12, then say: **Jesus makes it very clear that we'll be treated just as we treat others. We call this portion of Scripture the Golden Rule, and just as it applies to being kind to others, it applies to forgiveness, too.** Ask:

POWER POINTERS

Kids understand the concept of "if you will, I will" and vice versa. Help them realize that if we forgive others, they'll be more likely to forgive us—and God surely will!

★ **Whose forgiveness is Jesus talking about: someone else's or God's or both? Explain.**

★ **Why is it important to receive forgiveness from others? from God?**

★ **Is saying "I'm sorry" enough to be forgiven? Why or why not?**

Say: **When we say "I'm sorry," that tells others we need forgiveness. But we also have to change our ways to show we really mean we're sorry. Forgiveness is like the two sides of a coin. Just as every coin has a heads and a tails, so forgiveness has two sides. Heads, we want to give forgiveness, and tails, we want to be forgiven! Let's play a lively game of Decision Dominoes as we learn more about forgiving others and being forgiven.**

THE MESSAGE IN MOTION

Before class, make sure you have a set of at least twenty-five dominoes for each group of kids. You'll be forming four groups with your class. You'll also need a treat for each child, such as small wrapped candies, boxes of raisins, pencils, or erasers.

Have kids form four groups. Hand each group twenty-five to thirty dominoes, making sure that each group has the same number. Have children go to

the four corners of the room and tell them that this is a game of choices and decisions. In this game, they'll have only three minutes to stand their dominoes up in a line to topple later. Kids can choose to help another group stand their dominoes up, work on their own, or, if they notice one team is about to finish, tumble a few dominoes to delay them. Point out that the winning team will receive special treats.

As the race progresses, observe which groups are helping, hindering, or simply lining up their dominoes. You may discover many teachable moments during this game! And you'll be awarding treats first to those teams who helped others, forgave others, or treated others as they wanted to be treated. You'll end by giving everyone a treat.

When three minutes are up, call time and have everyone come to the center of the room. (Don't topple the dominoes yet!) Ask:

★ **How did your group do? Did you help anyone? hinder anyone's progress?**

★ **If you helped another group, why did you do that?**

★ **If you toppled someone's dominoes, did you decide to ask for forgiveness? If so, were you forgiven?**

★ **In what ways did you treat others as you wanted to be treated?**

★ **How did knowing the Golden Rule and what Jesus said about forgiveness affect your choices?**

Say: **In this game, forgiveness could prove to be very valuable. I mentioned that I had special treats for the winning team! Well, here they are!** Award the treats to the groups that helped, forgave, or treated others with kindness (which might be all the groups!). If any group toppled dominoes, give them treats in a moment.

Say: **In this game, speed wasn't everything! The winning group was the one that showed forgiveness or treated others the way they wanted to be treated.** Pause. **But since we're all winners in learning about forgiving, I have treats for everyone!** Hand out any remaining treats, then have kids give each other high fives.

Say: **I'm glad so many of you made good choices during the domino game. You're really learning about the right way to treat others. Our new Mighty Memory Verse is a good verse to teach us how we are to treat others, because it tells us that what goes around comes around— like a domino effect!** Let kids topple their dominoes.

SUPER SCRIPTURE

Have kids open their Bibles to Luke 6:37. Choose several volunteers to read the verse aloud, then say: **Our Mighty Memory Verse teaches us three things. What are they?** Lead children to recognize that the verse instructs us not to judge others, not to condemn others, and to be forgiving of others.

Say: **It's not always easy to forgive, is it? Sometimes we're angry and don't want to hear "I'm sorry." Or sometimes we're too**

busy blaming someone else to offer forgiveness. But God's Word tells us to be forgiving—not to judge, not to condemn or blame, but to forgive instead. Why is this good advice?

Allow kids to tell their ideas, then say: **Let's form three groups. One group will say, "Do not judge, and you will not be judged." The next group will say, "Do not condemn, and you will not be condemned." The third group will say, "Forgive, and you will be forgiven." After we repeat the verse two times, we'll switch roles.**

Continue repeating the verse two times each, switching roles until each group has repeated each of the parts. Then have kids get the boomerangs. Have kids use markers to write the word *judge* on the boomerangs, then circle it and draw a slash through the word to signify "Do not judge." Do the same with the word *condemn*. Finally, have children write the word *forgive* and draw a heart around it. After the words are written, challenge several kids to repeat the verse just by looking at their boomerangs.

Say: **Isn't God's Word great? It teaches us so many important truths and helps us live more like Jesus! I know you'll have this verse learned**

in no time—and your boomerangs will help. But right now, let's use our boomerangs to offer a special promise and prayer to God to let him know that we want to be forgiving so we'll be forgiven.

A **POWERFUL** PROMISE

Have kids sit in a circle holding the boomerangs. Ask for a moment of silence, then say: **We've discovered today that God wants us to be forgiving so we can be forgiven by others and by him. We've also learned that when we treat others with forgiveness, it will come back to us. We've worked on a new Mighty Memory Verse that teaches us not to judge or condemn others, but to forgive them. Luke 6:37 says,** (pause and encourage kids to repeat the verse with you) **"Do not judge, and you will not be judged. Do not condemn, and you will not be condemned. Forgive, and you will be forgiven."**

Hold up the Bible and say: **God promises that when we forgive others, we will be forgiven. What a wonderful promise—and one we all need! Let's make a promise of our own to God. We can each commit to being forgiving this week and to being willing to say "I'm sorry" so we can be forgiven, too. As we pass the Bible around our circle, we can make our own special promises. We can say, "I want to be forgiving, God, so I can be forgiven."** Pass the Bible until everyone has had a chance to hold it. Then share a prayer thanking God for his forgiveness and asking for God's help in having more forgiving spirits. End with a corporate "amen."

Have kids stand in place in the circle and hold their boomerangs. Say: **Let's end our time with a rhyme. We'll pass our boomerangs around the circle and repeat this rhyme.**

F-O-R-G-I-V-E!
I'll forgive you, and you'll forgive me.
That's how God planned it all to be.
F-O-R-G-I-V-E!

When your boomerang makes it back to you, silently think of one thing you can tell God you're sorry for and need forgiveness for. Then we'll pass the boomerangs one more time as you think of someone who might need your forgiveness.

Continue passing the boomerangs until you've passed them twice around the circle, then close by saying: **We all need forgiveness, and we all need to say we're sorry when we do and say wrong things. Let's keep our promises to God this week and be more forgiving of others because** (toss your boomerang in the air) **what goes around comes around!**

End with this responsive good-bye:

Leader: **May God's forgiveness be with you.**

Children: **And also with you!**

Distribute the Power Page! take-home papers as kids are leaving. Thank children for coming and encourage them to keep their promises to God this week.

POWER PAGE!

Suppose ... your best friend was upset because you broke his best pencil by mistake. Draw what you would do.

Now suppose ... the school bully needs forgiveness for pushing you. Draw what you would do. How is it different from the first picture? Why?

Color in each letter found in the word *forgiveness*. What do you see? It takes a LOT of this to forgive you and me!

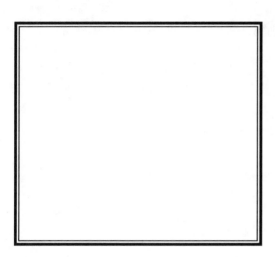

C	M	Z	X	D	P	L	B	U	A	C
X	L	V	i	L	M	T	V	G	X	B
B	O	Q	D	R	T	i	U	B	i	M
C	R	L	X	U	F	X	C	H	S	C
A	S	B	Y	D	U	C	Q	U	F	L
Y	i	M	D	M	X	H	Z	Y	G	K
P	E	T	X	L	A	T	U	T	E	D
H	V	T	B	C	T	X	D	A	O	H
Q	L	O	L	Q	H	B	L	V	T	Y
X	T	C	F	D	M	X	N	C	U	B
U	A	L	X	N	T	R	Y	D	Q	L
T	X	M	U	L	i	M	U	M	X	T

Forms of Forgiveness

Look in your Bible to find the many ways to say forgive and write them on the spaces.

Mark 11:25 _____

Luke 6:37 _____

Ephesians 1:7 _____

Ephesians 4:32 _____

Luke 7:49 _____

Psalm 78:38 _____

FOREVER FORGIVEN

Jesus died so we could be forgiven.

1 Corinthians 15:3-8
1 John 1:8–2:2, 12

SESSION SUPPLIES

★ Bibles
★ heavy stones
★ a large match box and cardboard
★ white and black paper hearts
★ felt and tacky craft glue
★ scissors and markers
★ sequins, glitter glue, and paint pens
★ photocopies of Luke 6:37 from page 126
★ photocopies of the poem from page 125
★ photocopies of the Power Page! (page 105)

MIGHTY MEMORY VERSE

Do not judge, and you will not be judged. Do not condemn, and you will not be condemned. Forgive, and you will be forgiven. Luke 6:37

(For older kids, add in Ephesians 1:7: "In him we have redemption through his blood, the forgiveness of sins, in accordance with the riches of God's grace.")

SESSION OBJECTIVES

During this session, children will
★ understand that we all need forgiveness of sins
★ realize that Jesus can forgive us through his death
★ know that forgiveness was part of God's plan
★ express thanks to Jesus for his forgiveness

BIBLE BACKGROUND

Forgive. What an interesting word, especially when we look at the two words that combine to make up forgive: *for* and *give*. It's easy to see how this wonderful word came to mean all that Jesus lived and died for—and so much more! *For* us, Jesus came to *give* his love. *For* us, Jesus came to *give* his life. It was *for* us that Jesus came to *give* instruction, healing, help, and assurance of God's abiding presence. And Jesus came to *forgive* us of sin so we could live in heaven eternally at peace with God! Christ's forgiveness isn't merely an act of pardon in our lives—it's a celebration of everlasting love!

Kids know when they've messed up. They know when someone is angry with them for doing or saying wrong things. And children experience feelings of shame, unhappiness, guilt, and misery associated with sin. Help kids learn the wonderful truth about Jesus' forgiveness and how it's available to all who accept him into their hearts and lives. Share with your kids the wondrous celebration of Christ's love and forgiveness as you explore what Jesus did for us on the cross and beyond!

POWER FOCUS

Before class, gather one or two heavy stones for each child. You'll use the stones for a project during the lesson.

Have each child choose one or two heavy stones. Instruct kids to stand in a circle with their arms outstretched at their sides, holding the stone or stones in their hands. Tell kids to remain standing with outstretched arms until you tell them to put their arms down.

Then say: **Last week we began exploring forgiveness and how we need to forgive others so that we can be forgiven. But sometimes we think that we don't need to be forgiven for things we've done or said. We might think others need to be forgiven but not us. But the Bible tells us we've all sinned and need forgiveness.**

Tell kids to keep holding their stones, then read aloud Romans 3:23. Continue: **Our sins weigh us down like the heavy stones you're holding. Sin in our lives is heavy and uncomfortable—even painful. So how do we get rid of the heavy burden of sin? How can we be forgiven? Through Jesus' love! Today we'll be learning about how Jesus forgave our sins through his death on the cross, which is the shape you are standing in. Through Jesus' death, we can all be forgiven and have new lives! Now set down your stones and relax your arms.**

Pause for kids to respond, then say: **Ahh ... that feels better, doesn't it? And that's how it is when we feel Jesus' love and forgiveness!** Ask:

★ **How can sin affect our lives? how we see others? ourselves? God?**

★ **How is Jesus' forgiveness a demonstration of his love?**

Say: **Those stones were heavy and a bit painful. But they help remind us of how heavy our lives are when we don't have Jesus' forgiveness!**

Today we'll discover why each of us needs Christ's forgiveness and how we can have his forgiveness. We'll learn that forgiveness was part of God's plan for the world. And we'll thank Jesus for his incredible love. Now let's read what the Bible tells us about Jesus' love and how he died to forgive our sins. Set the stones aside until later.

THE MIGHTY MESSAGE

Before class, prepare a match box with a secret hiding place. Use a large kitchen match box and carefully tape a false back in the match box. Cut a piece of cardboard that resembles the match box to the same height and width as the end flap of the box. Tape it carefully in place down the center inside to make two compartments. (See illustration on page 101.)

You'll also need to cut out a white paper heart and a black paper heart. Make the paper hearts about 1-inch across. Slide the white heart into one compartment, but remember which compartment it's in! During the activity, you'll be sliding the match box halfway open and quickly showing kids the empty side of the box as you slide the black paper heart inside that compartment. As you talk, slyly turn the box around so the white heart will be revealed when you slide open the box a second time. Kids will be amazed and think the black heart has become white! Quickly set the box aside so the hidden black heart won't be discovered.

Gather kids and hold the match box with the empty side facing them. (Be sure you've hidden the white heart inside the back compartment—and don't forget where it is!) Hold up the black heart and say: **Before Jesus forgave us, our hearts were full of sin and sadness. What kinds of things did people do before Jesus' love and forgiveness came to us?**

Allow kids to name things such as saying unkind words, telling lies, disobeying God, and ignoring the Bible. Then say: **Our sinful natures made God so sad.** Place the black heart in the box and slide the box closed. As you continue, slyly rotate the box so the side containing the white heart ends up facing the kids. Continue: **God wanted us to be his friends again and to live with him in** heaven. God knew we needed forgiveness, so God set his plan in motion. God sent his only Son, Jesus, to love us, to teach us, and to forgive us! And even though some people didn't think they needed forgiveness, they certainly did! Jesus died on the cross for the sins of the entire world so we could be forgiven and have clean, new lives and pure hearts!

Slide the match box open and remove the white heart. Then quickly continue as you set the match box to the side: **Listen to what the Bible says Jesus did for us.** Read aloud 1 Corinthians 15:3-8 and 1 John 1:8–2:2, 12. Then ask:

★ **In what ways did Jesus demonstrate his love for us on the cross?**

★ **Why did God want us to be forgiven?**

★ **When we love Jesus and are forgiven, how do our lives change?**

★ **How can we receive Jesus' forgiveness?**

Say: **When we love Jesus and accept him into our hearts and lives, he promises to forgive us. We all need to be forgiven, and there's only one person who can do this for us. We can't forgive our own sins—only Jesus can do this for us! Isn't it wonderful to know that Jesus loved us enough to pay for our sins so we can be forgiven? Let's have a little review with a game of Who, What, Where, Why, and How. I'll ask a question. When you think you know the answer, put your finger on your nose.**

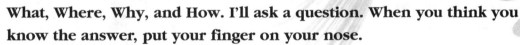

Ask the following questions and allow children to give their answers to each. Remember that the questions may have several answers!

★ **Who needs forgiveness?** (All of us)

★ **What did Jesus bring us?** (Love and forgiveness; salvation)

★ **Where does forgiveness begin?** (With admitting our sins; with Jesus' love)

★ **Why did Jesus forgive our sins?** (So we could live forever; so we could live with God; because he loved us; because it was part of God's plan)

★ **How can we be forgiven?** (Ask for Jesus' forgiveness; admit our sins; love and follow Jesus; be baptized)

Say: **Remember our heavy stones and how it felt so good to have that burden gone when we set them down? That's what our hearts feel like** when we have Jesus' love and forgiveness! We feel lighter, happier, and ready to follow Jesus! In fact, we feel like the doors to heaven just swung open even wider! Let's make our stones into cool doorstops to hold our doors at home wide open. They'll remind us that with Jesus' love and forgiveness, the doors to heaven are open and welcoming us!

THE MESSAGE IN MOTION

Before class, make a copy of the Scripture strip for Luke 6:37 (page 126) for each child. Cut the strips apart.

Have each child choose a stone. Show children how to cut small pieces of felt and then glue them to the bottoms of the stones to protect the surfaces the stones rest on. Glue the Scripture strips of Luke 6:37 to the felt on the bottom of the stones. Then invite kids to use markers, glitter glue, sequins, and paint pens to decorate the stones.

As kids work, encourage them to name ways our lives change when we receive Jesus' forgiveness. Lead them to mention that we speak kind words, read the Bible, help others, obey God, and follow Jesus in all we do and say. Have kids write the words "Jesus forgives us" on their stones.

When the doorstopper stones are complete, say: **Keep your stone by your door and use them to hold the door open. Each time you look at your special stone, say a word of thanks to Jesus for removing the heaviness of sin in your life and replacing it with love, lightness, and forgiveness.**

Last week we learned that we need to forgive others so we can be forgiven. Jesus wants us to be forgiving so that we too can be forgiven and live with him forever in heaven. And our memory verse helps us learn to be more forgiving each day. Let's line our stones up on the floor and use them to help us review our Mighty Memory Verse as we learn even more about the gift of forgiveness.

SUPER SCRIPTURE

Have kids line the stones down the center of the room and about two feet apart. Then gather the kids into two groups and have groups stand at opposite ends of the stones. Explain to kids that in this review of Luke 6:37, one child from each group will hop up to a stone and take turns repeating portions of the verse. For example, after both kids hop up to the first stone, the player from line one is to say "Do not judge." Then both kids hop up to another stone, and the hopper in line two says, "and you will not be judged." Have kids continue hopping and repeating portions of the verse until the entire verse has been recited.

After the verse has been repeated, have the next two kids in line begin hopping. Continue until everyone has had a chance to hop beside the stones and repeat the verse. (If you have older kids, be sure to use the additional verse if you've chosen to work on it as well.)

Then gather children in a group and say: **What is this verse telling us? In other words, what can we learn from this verse to help us every day?** Allow kids to share their ideas, then ask:

★ **How can not judging others help us? help others?**

★ **In what ways can not blaming others make us more understanding and compassionate?**

★ **Who is someone you can be more forgiving to this week?**

Say: **God's Word is not only good to learn, it's important to understand. When we understand what God is telling us, we can put his teaching to work in our lives. God's Word in Luke 6:37 warns us about judging and condemning others and tells us to be forgiving so we can be forgiven. What other things can we apply this same rule to?**

Help kids brainstorm rules such as "Don't gossip, and you will not be gossiped about" and "Be kind, and you will be shown kindness." Repeat the verse in unison two more times and be sure to repeat the reference with the verse.

Say: **God promises to forgive us if we forgive others and if we accept Jesus into our lives. Those are special promises we can count on because God always keeps his promises! Let's make our own promise to God, then we'll offer a prayer thanking Jesus for his love and forgiveness.**

A POWERFUL PROMISE

Before class, make a copy of the poem from page 125 for each child. For a nice touch, use colored or design photocopy paper.

Have kids sit in a circle and ask for a moment of silence, then say: **We learned today that all of us need God's forgiveness and that God provided** a way for us to be forgiven through his Son, Jesus. We also discovered that Jesus died for our sins and that we will be forgiven when we accept Jesus into our hearts and lives. Finally, we reviewed the Mighty Memory Verse from Luke 6:37, which says, (pause and invite kids to repeat the verse with you).

Hold up the Bible and say: **We know that God's plan for forgiveness is through Jesus and that when we know, love, and follow Jesus, we can have his forgiveness and eternal life with God!**

What a powerful promise that is! Let's make a promise of our own to God right now. We can admit our wrongs and tell Jesus we want him to live in our hearts and lives. As we pass the Bible around our circle, we can make our own special promises. We can silently say, "I'm sorry, Jesus, and I want you to be Lord of my life!"

Pass the Bible until everyone has had a chance to hold it. Then offer a prayer thanking Jesus for his incredible love and for his sacrifice on the cross so that we could be forgiven and live eternally with him in heaven. End with a corporate "amen."

Say: **It's important to express our thanks and love for the sacrifice Jesus made when he died on the cross so we could be forgiven. We've thanked Jesus through making doorstop stones to remind us of his loving forgiveness, and we've thanked Jesus through our powerful promise and prayer. What are some other ways we can express our thanks to Jesus?**

Lead kids to suggest ways such as obeying Jesus, telling others about his love and forgiveness, and even singing our thank-you's. Then say: **I have a short poem for us to share as another way of expressing our love to Jesus.** Hand each child a copy of "Why Did Jesus Have to Die?" Read the poem once in unison, then have four groups each read a different line, with everyone reading the last line together.

Say: **Put your poem on or under your pillow so you can read it each night before you go to sleep and each morning as you awaken. Take a few moments to read the poem, then thank Jesus for his love and forgiveness as you promise to follow and obey him all day.** End with this responsive good-bye:

Leader: **May Jesus' love and forgiveness be with you.**

Children: **And also with you!**

Distribute the Power Page! take-home papers as kids are leaving. Remind kids to take home their poems and doorstop stones. Thank kids for coming and encourage them to keep their promises to God this week.

POWER PAGE!

Check it out... There's forgiveness for you and me!

Check the sentences that tell what we must do in order to receive Jesus' forgiveness.

- ❏ Admit we need forgiveness.
- ❏ Ask Jesus to help us change.
- ❏ Earn Jesus' love by being good.
- ❏ Ask Jesus to live in our lives.
- ❏ Never change our old ways.
- ❏ Be baptized.
- ❏ Deny that we've ever sinned.

HOT CROSS BUNS

Here's a traditional Easter treat to make and eat!

You'll need a bag of rolls, white tube icing, and tiny red-hot candies.

Place the rolls on a platter and use the icing to make a cross on the top of each roll. Add a red candy in the center to remind you how Jesus forgave our sins on the cross through his blood and his love. Enjoy!

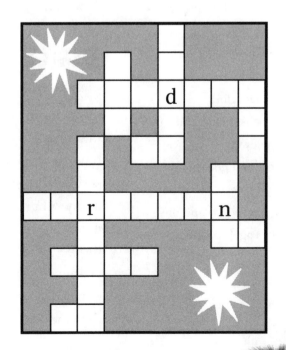

SEEK-N-SEARCH

Use your Bible to fill in the missing words to Luke 6:37. Then fit the words into the seek-n-search puzzle.

Do _____ _____, and _____ will not _____ judged. _____ not _____, _____ you will not _____ condemned. _____, and you _____ be _____.

105

THE CHALLENGE TO CHANGE

When we're forgiven, we change our ways.

Acts 9:1-18
1 Corinthians 15:9, 10
2 Corinthians 5:17

SESSION SUPPLIES

★ Bibles
★ two bags containing jewelry, neckties, mittens, scarves, sunglasses, and other items of apparel
★ a small plastic mirror for each child
★ tacky craft glue
★ paint pens, glitter glue, and plastic jewels
★ scissors and gold braid
★ photocopies of the Whiz Quiz (page 114) and the Power Page! (page 113)

MIGHTY MEMORY VERSE

Do not judge, and you will not be judged. Do not condemn, and you will not be condemned. Forgive, and you will be forgiven. Luke 6:37

(For older kids, add in Ephesians 1:7: "In him we have redemption through his blood, the forgiveness of sins, in accordance with the riches of God's grace.")

SESSION OBJECTIVES

During this session, children will
★ understand what repentance means
★ realize that change comes from the inside
★ discover how to change through Christ's forgiveness
★ learn that Jesus' forgiveness is for everyone

BIBLE BACKGROUND

The times, they are a-changin'. These words to a popular folk song from a few years back reflected on the changes in a changing world of that time. But it's not so much the times as it is attitudes that need changin' when it comes to serving Christ. Zacchaeus, Mary Magdalene, Peter, and many others discovered that through Jesus' love and forgiveness, their lives, attitudes, and actions had changed for the better in miraculous ways. Perhaps the most astounding changes occurred inside of Paul when he experienced his conversion on the road to Damascus and turned into a dynamo for Christ and his church. It is truly amazing that the faithful, forgiving, and loving attitudes of God and Jesus never change but lead us to change in the most wondrous of ways!

Kids love the excitement of change! Whether it's the seasons to changing grades in school, kids thrive on newness. What a grand lesson for children to learn as they discover the exciting changes that Jesus' love and forgiveness bring into our hearts and minds. Invite your kids to explore the positive changes that come with living in Christ's forgiveness and thus discover how their actions, attitudes, and values become new and help them to serve Jesus even better!

POWER FOCUS

Before class, gather five or six simple apparel or accessory items—such as clip-on earrings, necklaces, a ring, a small bow, scarves, gloves, a hat, or a handkerchief—in a bag. You will need another bag with the same number of items, but you won't use the second bag until later in the lesson.

To begin, place the bag beside you and gather kids. Explain that you want to see how observant they are today, then instruct them to sit with their backs facing you. Quickly don something from the bag and have kids turn around and see if they can tell what you changed about your appearance. Repeat this several times, then invite several children to change their appearances.

After kids have guessed all the changes, say: **That was fun, wasn't it? It's fun to change our appearances with clothing, accessories, or even things such as glasses, hair color, or fancy jewelry. But these are outside changes. They have nothing to do with the way we are on the inside.** Ask:

★ **Is change good? Explain.**

★ **What are changes people sometimes make on the inside?**

★ **Why do you think people might change the way they feel on the inside?**

Say: **Change can be a very good thing—especially when it makes us more like Jesus! Today we'll be learning about being changed from the inside out. We'll also discover that when Jesus forgives us, we become changed in special ways. And we'll learn about what it means to repent** and what changes take place in our lives when we're truly sorry for things we've done. Right now, let's listen to a Bible story about a man who changed for the better on the inside because of the Lord's forgiveness.

THE MIGHTY MESSAGE

Have children sit in a circle and place the two bags of apparel items beside you. Say: **Sometimes we change our attitudes or change our minds about something or someone. Have you ever found that you like a food you used to think was icky? Or have you ever discovered you really liked a person you thought was unfriendly?** Encourage kids to tell about times they may have changed their minds or attitudes for the better.

Say: **It's a good thing we can change our minds, attitudes, and actions, because sometimes our original ones need changing! Our Bible lesson today is about a man whose original attitudes and actions needed to change and about how Jesus helped them change for the better. We'll use our bags of silly accessories to help us tell the message. We'll pass the bags around the circle. Whenever you hear the word *change* or *changed*, stop passing the bags, then whoever is holding a bag can quickly put on something from inside before beginning to pass the bag again.**

Start passing a bag in each direction, then say: **After Jesus died to forgive our sins and was risen from death, many of his followers began meeting to share about Jesus and to tell others about him. But a man named Saul did not love Jesus and did not believe he was God's Son. Saul just wouldn't *change* his mind or his heart! In fact, Saul devoted his life to hurting people who loved and followed Jesus. He wouldn't *change* from the mean guy he was!**

Then one day, Saul was traveling on the road to Damascus. The road had never *changed*—it was still dusty and bumpy. Saul was on his way to Damascus to capture and hurt Jesus' followers there. Oh, would Saul ever

POWER POINTERS

Help kids identify with people in the Bible who experienced great changes in their attitudes and actions. Include reviews of Zacchaeus, Jonah, and Peter if you have time!

change? Then all of a sudden, the sky *changed!* There was a blinding light from heaven that flashed around Saul, and he fell to the ground. Saul heard Jesus asking why Saul hated him so. Jesus told Saul to go to Damascus. But when Saul got up, his eyesight had *changed!* Saul was blind.

But Saul obeyed Jesus and went to the home of a man named Ananias. Ananias told him that Jesus would *change* him and even fill him with the Holy Spirit. And suddenly, Saul's sight *changed* again—he could see! From that moment on, Saul *changed!* He loved Jesus and followed him. Soon Saul's name was *changed* to Paul. And for the rest of Paul's *changed* life, he helped establish the church all over the world, teaching others to love and change for Jesus too!

Set the bags down and say: **Paul was changed in a miraculous way, wasn't he? His attitude, life, mind, and heart were changed for Jesus, and he didn't continue doing the things he did in his old life. I see that some of you are changed by what you're wearing.** Ask:

★ **How are inside changes better than just changing our appearance?**

★ **In what ways can change help us grow closer to Jesus? closer to others?**

★ **Could Paul have done the same things he did without changing for Jesus? Explain.**

★ **In what ways did Jesus help change Paul?**

★ **If Jesus could forgive Paul, can he forgive anyone? Explain.**

Have kids return the apparel items to the bags as you say: **Jesus knew the awful things Paul had done, and Jesus knew the great things Paul could do if he was loved and forgiven. So Jesus forgave Paul on the road to Damascus. Jesus' forgiveness is for anyone who wants it—even for Paul!**

Paul was so thankful when he was changed by Jesus' forgiveness and by Jesus' gift of the Holy Spirit. Because Paul loved Jesus, he was sorry for all that he had done and wanted to change his attitudes and his actions. And just look at how Paul changed! He spent the rest of his life loving and following Jesus and helping others change for Jesus too! Paul established many churches, taught fellow Christians, and wrote letters that we call the epistles in the Bible. Wow! Now that's change! Listen to what Paul wrote about his change to the church in Corinth. Read aloud 1 Corinthians 15:9, 10. Then ask:

★ **How can we change the way we feel through Jesus' forgiveness?**

★ **Which is better: changing the outside of us or changing the inside? Explain.**

★ **What attitudes and actions do we have when we change for Jesus?**

Read aloud 2 Corinthians 5:17, then say: **When we tell Jesus we're sorry, we repent. But with true repentance comes change. We speak with kind new words, we're more helpful and thoughtful to others, and we joyously tell them about Jesus and his forgiving love. In other words, we change our attitudes and our actions for Jesus! Let's play a lively relay to remind us that with forgiveness comes change.**

THE MESSAGE IN MOTION

Place the two bags of wearing apparel at one end of the room and have kids form two groups at the opposite end of the room. Instruct the groups to stand in lines and explain that in this relay race, the first person in each line will hop to a bag and put on three of the items while everyone else on the team has eyes closed. Then those players must hop back to their lines to see if their team members can guess the changes made. When all three changes have been identified, the players must hop back and remove the items and return to tag the second players in line. Continue until all players have had a chance to change.

Have kids sit in a group and ask them why it's easier to change outside appearances than to change on the inside. Then say: **Changing on the inside and having it show on the outside isn't always easy. It's sometimes easier to want to fall back into our old behaviors. When we repent, it means we're sorry and truly want to change. Remember our lesson about Zacchaeus a few weeks ago? He's a great example of change! And we also learned a couple of weeks ago that saying "I'm sorry" isn't enough—we need to change our ways and not repeat old behaviors. And that's not always easy. That's why when Jesus forgives us, he sends the Holy Spirit to help us change and stay changed for good!** Ask:

★ **In what ways can the Holy Spirit help us?**

★ **How can we ask the Holy Spirit's help if we need it?**

Say: **Saying "I'm sorry" is the first step. Then inviting Jesus to live in our hearts and minds comes next. And after receiving Jesus' forgiveness, we show we've changed through Jesus' love and the help of the Holy Spirit. No wonder change feels so good! Let's read once more what the Bible tells us about having new, changed lives through Jesus.**

Read aloud 2 Corinthians 5:17, then say: **God's Word can help us stay changed in our new lives by teaching us and by giving us perfect advice! Let's review more of God's Word with our Mighty Memory Verse.**

SUPER SCRIPTURE

Before class, cut the gold braid into 3-inch and 2-inch lengths. Cut one of each length for every child.

Gather kids and repeat the Mighty Memory Verse three times in unison. If you have older kids, also repeat the extra challenge verse (Ephesians 1:7) three times in unison. Be sure to include the Scripture references as you repeat the verses.

Then say: **You're all learning the Mighty Memory Verse so well! We learn God's Word so we can understand what it says. And when we understand God's Word, we can put it to use in our lives. How can this verse help us become more forgiving of others?**

Encourage kids to tell their ideas, then say: **We've been learning that when Jesus forgives us, we become changed. The Mighty Memory Verse reminds us that some of those changes include not judging others, not condemning or blaming others, and being more forgiving. These are good changes to have in our lives! What are other changes we want to have?**

Allow time for kids to share their thoughts. Suggestions might include being more kind to others, not gossiping, always telling the truth, reading the Bible to learn more about God and Jesus, and praying more. Then say: **When we look in a mirror, we might not look like we've changed. But when we love Jesus and have his forgiveness in our lives, we are changed! Let's make fun mirrors to remind us that every time we look in the mirror, we see changes for Jesus—on the inside!**

Distribute the plastic mirrors and show kids how to glue gold braid in the shape of a cross on the glass. Then invite kids to use glitter glue, plastic jewels, and paint pens to decorate the mirrors. Help kids write the words "Be changed for Jesus!" on the handles or on the back of the mirrors.

When the mirrors are finished, say: **Each time you look into a mirror, be glad that you know the changes from Jesus' forgiveness are inside you and**

thank Jesus for his special love! Right now, let's thank Jesus for his love as we make a promise and share a prayer.

A POWERFUL PROMISE

Have kids sit in a circle, ask for a moment of silence, and say: **We've learned today that Jesus' love and forgiveness change us for the better. We've learned that changes come on the inside and show up through our actions and words. We know that Jesus' love and forgiveness are for anyone who wants it. And we've reviewed our Mighty Memory Verse, which says,** (pause and encourage children to repeat the verse with you).

Hold up the Bible and say: **Jesus promises that his forgiveness is for all who seek it and for all those who will accept him into their lives. That's Jesus' promise! Let's make a promise of our own. We can each commit to changing for Jesus and trying to follow and obey him more closely. As we pass the Bible around our circle, we can make our own special promises. We can say, "I want to change for you, Jesus!"**

Pass the Bible until everyone has had a chance to hold it. Then invite kids to chant the lively action rhyme below to the rhythm of the military sound-off march. Encourage children to act out the changes our eyes can see, then cover their hearts for the last line.

I can change the way I stand—(*stand in funny poses*)
Change the way I clap my hands! (*clap in unusual ways*)
I can change the way I sit—(*sit in silly positions*)
Change my smile, and this is it! (*smile in comical ways*)
But the best change our eyes can't see (*march in place and close eyes*)
Is the loving change inside of me! (*open eyes and cover hearts*)

Before kids leave, allow five or ten minutes to complete the Whiz Quiz from page 114. If you run out of time, be sure to complete this page first thing next week. The Whiz Quiz is an invaluable tool that allows kids, teachers, and parents to see what kids have learned in the previous three weeks.

End with this responsive good-bye:

Leader: **May Jesus' love be with you.**

Children: **And also with you!**

Distribute the Power Page! take-home papers as children are leaving and remind them to take home their mirrors. Thank kids for coming and encourage them to keep their promises to God this week.

POWER PAGE!

POWER OF CHANGE!

When Jesus came into Saul's life, he really changed! Even Saul's name changed to Paul. Here are other names that were changed by God's touch! Can you find them all?

Sa(u)l ———————➤ Paul (Acts 13:19)

Abram ———————➤ _ _ _ _ _ _ _
(Genesis 17:5)

(S)arai ———————➤ ◯ _ _ _ _
(Genesis 17:15)

(J)acob ———————➤ _ _ _ _ _ _
(Genesis 32:28)

Simon ———————➤ ◯ _ _ _
(Matthew 16:18)

Now unscramble the circled letters to complete the sentence.

When _ _ _ _ _ _ touches us, we become changed!

OLD TO NEW

Make this cool cleanser to change old pennies to new! You'll need:
- ★ ¼ cup lemon juice
- ★ ⅛ cup water
- ★ an old toothbrush
- ★ baking soda
- ★ pennies
- ★ a soft towel

Directions: Mix the lemon juice and water. Dip the toothbrush in the lemon water, then in the baking soda. Scrub the pennies. Rinse the pennies with water and rub them with the soft towel. Wow, they shine like new!

Show everyone you're a new cretion in Jesus by serving through your own cleaning service! Use your cool cleanser to shine up chrome bumpers, hat racks, silverware, and hubcaps. (Be sure to rinse items with water and buff them dry with the soft towel!)

Crazy Circuit Board

Follow the arrows to plug in the missing letters to this puzzle from Luke 6:37.

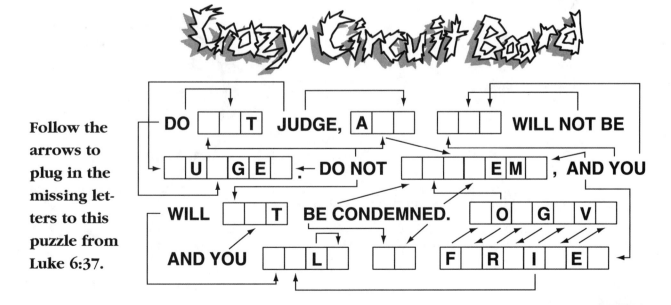

DO [ ][ ]T JUDGE, A[ ][ ] [ ][ ][ ] WILL NOT BE

[ ]U[ ]GE[ ]. ◄— DO NOT [ ][ ][ ][ ]EM[ ] , AND YOU

WILL [ ][ ]T BE CONDEMNED. [ ]O[ ]G[ ]V[ ]

AND YOU [ ][ ]L [ ][ ][ ] F[ ]R[ ]IE[ ]

WHIZ QUIZ

Draw lines to connect the dots at the end of questions with their correct answers. Then read the letters the lines cross to discover who we're to forgive.

WHO forgave our sins? •

WHAT does forgiveness show? •

WHEN are we to forgive others? •

WHERE did Jesus die for us? •

WHY did Jesus die? •

HOW can we have Jesus' forgiveness? •

L T G O E R H J S O

• our love

• on the cross

• to forgive our sins

• ask and accept Jesus

• Jesus

• all the time

Use the words from the word bank to fill in the spaces to the Mighty Memory Verse.

Do ___ ___ ___ judge, and ___ ___ ___ will not be ___ ___ ___ ___ ___ ___.
     12   8   1   9   4

___ ___ not ___ ___ ___ ___ ___ ___ ___, ___ ___ ___ you will
              5   14

___ ___ ___ be condemned. ___ ___ ___ ___ ___ ___ ___ ___, and
                              7   16   2   17

you ___ ___ ___ ___ be ___ ___ ___ ___ ___ ___ ___.
     10   3   11 15

Forgive   forgiven
judged   condemn
will   and   not
   not   Do
      you

What are we to do? Fill in the letters in the correct spaces.

___ ___ ___ ___ ___ ___ ___   ___ ___ ___ ___ ___ ___ ___ ___
 7   1   3   9 10   2   5   15 11   4 16   8 12 14 17

REVIEW LESSON

Your attitude should be
the same as that of
Christ Jesus,
Philippians 2:5

VALUE SEEKERS

Let's seek to have the values of Jesus!

Philippians 2:5-11

SESSION SUPPLIES

★ Bibles
★ construction paper
★ scissors and tape
★ markers and crayons
★ tacky craft glue
★ plastic jewels and a pie pan
★ a small box for each child
★ plastic bowls and spoons
★ ice cream and toppings
★ photocopies of all the
  Scripture strips (page 126)

MIGHTY MEMORY VERSE

This is a review lesson of all four previous verses: Psalm 119:105; Ephesians 4:32; Psalm 100:4; and Luke 6:37.

SESSION OBJECTIVES

During this session, children will
★ recognize values we need in our lives
★ review the values Jesus taught us
★ understand that values become a natural part of our lives
★ thank God for help in nurturing positive values

BIBLE BACKGROUND

Whether in biblical or modern days, having certain values has always been the way we treasure important attitudes in our lives. Values determine how we treat others, what we think about ourselves, and how we view God and his saving grace through Jesus. Values separate heroes from has-beens, moral champions from moral misfits. And Christian values such as truth, honesty, forgiveness, love, and kindness heal the sick, feed the poor, and change the world for Christ. Jesus lived and demonstrated every value we're to nurture in our own lives, and through his model and perfect examples, we're transformed into having the mind and heart of Christ as we grow closer to God and each other.

Can we ever teach enough solid values to our kids? At every turn and twist in their young lives, kids need strong role models to lean on and a real appreciation for the importance of Christ-centered values—as well as the consequences of not having them. Use this lesson as a powerful review to sum up what children have learned in the past weeks as they gain confidence in living and thinking as Christ did.

POWER FOCUS

Before class, cut out eight construction-paper hearts. Write one of the following words on each heart: truth, love, honesty, forgiveness, kindness, praise, change, and thankfulness.

To begin, gather kids and form seven groups. Hand each group a paper heart to hide somewhere in the class. Point out that the hiding places cannot be inside of or under an object but must be at least in partial view. As kids hide their hearts, slyly hide the eighth heart.

When the hearts are hidden, have kids sit in the center of the room and choose one group to be clappers and one group to be seekers. Have the clappers identify which heart they've hidden (truth, love, and so on). As the seekers search for the correct heart, the clappers will clap slowly if the seekers are far from the heart or quickly if they're nearing the hiding place. Continue until the seekers have located the heart, then have the clappers choose another group to clap and the seekers another group to seek.

Continue until all the paper hearts except yours have been found. Then turn all the kids into seekers until they find the last paper heart. Set the hearts aside for the Message in Motion game. Gather kids and ask:

★ **Why are values such as those written on the hearts important to seek out in our lives?**

★ **How do we develop these values?**

★ **What would our lives be like without honesty, love, thankfulness, and other values?**

★ **How are each of these values shown in Jesus' life?**

Say: **For the past several weeks we've been learning about each of these values and why each is important to God and us. We've learned about love and kindness, thankfulness and praise. We've explored for-**

giveness, change, truth, and honesty. Today we'll review these important values one more time and see if we can think of other values to grow in our lives. We'll review our Mighty Memory Verses and play a fun game to help us review them.

We're all value seekers on the trail of wonderful treasures that are ours with the values we grow in our lives. So let's go on a fun treasure hunt of values right now as we review what we've been learning. But first, you'll need treasure boxes!

Hand each child a small box to cover with construction paper and decorate with markers or crayons. (For an exciting touch, use shiny gold wrapping paper to cover the small boxes instead of construction paper!) Write the words "Values Treasure Chest" on the boxes. If you'd like, use tape to create a "hinge" for the back of the lid so it will open and close like a treasure box. When the boxes are complete, have each child cut out eight paper hearts and write the values on them as you did for the seek and find game.

POWER POINTERS

If you are able to, purchase a WWJD bracelet, key chain, or pencil for each child to remind kids that we want the same values as Jesus and to do what Jesus would do.

THE MIGHTY MESSAGE

Before class, place the plastic jewels on a pie pan (or a paper plate). You'll need several containers of tacky craft glue, and be sure to have at least ten plastic jewels for each child.

Have kids sit in a circle holding their treasure boxes and paper hearts. Set the tacky craft glue and jewels beside you. Then say: **In this review, we'll identify which values I'm describing. I'll give you hints from our lessons, and when you think you know which values I'm describing, hold a paper heart up high. Ready? God's Word is found in the Bible, and we can trust what it says. We know that God is honest, and he wants us to be truthful too in all we say and do! And the best part? The truth will set us free! What are the values?**

Have kids identify the values as truth and honesty. Invite kids to glue one jewel on a paper heart for truth and one on a heart for honesty, then slide them into their treasure chests.

Say: **That was fun! Now let's do another one. When Paul felt this from Jesus, he was different in a big way! We know that we have to do this for others, and then we can be forgiven. Jesus even died on the cross so he could do this for us. What values am I talking about?** Identify the values as forgiveness and change, then glue a jewel on a heart for forgiveness and another jewel on a heart for change.

Say: **You're doing so well! Here's the next one. Jesus healed ten lepers, but only one gave these to Jesus. It's important to tell God how wonderful he is and to give him honor and glory and these. What values am I thinking of?** Have kids identify the values as thankfulness and praise. Glue a jewel on the appropriate hearts.

Say: **Oh, how well you've learned our values! And now for the last two. Jesus did this for his disciples when he washed their feet. And when Jesus showed this to Zacchaeus, Zacchaeus gave the people's money back. We do this because God first loved us and because we want to be K-L-F for Jesus. Which values are these?** Have kids identify the values as love and kindness and glue jewels on their last two paper hearts. Then have kids slide the hearts into their treasure chests.

Say: **Wow! You all have treasure chests full of wonderful values God wants us to have in our lives!** Ask:

★ **In what ways are these values like treasures?**

★ **How do these values draw us closer to God? to others?**

★ **In what ways do these values make us feel better about ourselves?**

★ **How does having and using these values demonstrate our love for God? our obedience to him?**

Read aloud Philippians 2:5-11, then say: **When we develop these values in our lives, we become more like Jesus—and that makes God smile! The Bible teaches us that we should be just like Jesus and have the same values that he has so whatever we do or say is just what Jesus would do or say.** Ask:

★ **What are other values Jesus had that we can have in our own lives?**

Have children suggest other values such as loyalty, faithfulness, and trust. Then write those values on more paper hearts and glue on jewels to add to the treasure boxes.

When you're finished, say: **Keep your treasure box close to you and take out all the hearts each night before bed. Read and review the value on each heart and ask yourself if you demonstrated that value during the day. Then pray and ask for God's help in continuing to grow and show Jesus' values in your life every day. Now let's have a fun celebration with Servant Sundaes as we review more about our valuable values!** Set the treasure boxes aside until later.

THE MESSAGE IN MOTION

Set out ice cream, plastic bowls and spoons, and toppings. Have children find partners, then say: **During the past several weeks we've been learning about love, kindness, thankfulness, praise, forgiveness, and honesty. Did you know that each of these values can be demonstrated by serving God or others? Let's take turns serving our partners, then we'll discover how serving others is a powerful way to show so many of Jesus' values.**

Have kids take turns making and serving sundaes to their partners. Encourage kids to ask their partners what they would like, then remind partners to be thankful and show appreciation for the kind service being offered.

When everyone has a sundae, offer a blessing thanking God for his love and for the many ways we can demonstrate the values he wants us to have. As kids enjoy their treats, ask:

★ **How can kindness and love be shown through serving others and God?**

★ **In what ways can thankfulness and praise be demonstrated through serving?**

★ **How are forgiveness and change a way of serving others and God?**

★ **How are honesty and truth shown through serving God and others?**

Say: **Serving others is one of the main reasons Jesus came to earth. And through our own serving of others and God, we show that love, kindness, thankfulness, and all the other values are alive in our hearts! God's Word says "Serve one another in love" (Galatians 5:13). And we can model almost all of Jesus' values in our lives by remembering to serve one another and love each other every day. Now let's see just how much of God's Word we've learned with a fun review of our Mighty Memory Verses!** Toss the bowls and spoons in the trash and clean up any sticky hands.

SUPER SCRIPTURE

Before class, photocopy and cut out all the Scripture strips on page 126, one copy per child. Be sure to have Psalm 119:105; Ephesians 4:32; Psalm 100:4; and Luke 6:37. If you have older kids, also copy the extra verses they've been working on. For a festive touch, use colored or neon paper for the strips. You will also need access to an overhead projector and a blank transparency, a chalkboard, or a dry erase board. If you have none of these, use large sheets of poster board taped to the wall.

Hand each child a set of the Mighty Memory Verses. Read through each strip in unison, then have kids turn their Scripture strips face down. Give them a word or two to begin one of the verses and see if they can repeat the entire verse. Continue until you're reviewed each Mighty Memory Verse.

Then say: **God's Word is important to learn, understand, and use in our lives. We can't have one without all the others! Let's see how well you remember the verses. I'll draw spaces for the words to one of these verses on the board. You can guess a word from one of the verses. If that word goes into one of the blanks, you can come write it in the correct space. If the word isn't there, guess another one.**

Continue drawing spaces and letting kids fill in words until you've completed each verse. Then ask:

★ **In what ways does God's Word help us find and develop values in our lives?**

★ **How can using God's Word every day strengthen those values? our faith? our obedience and love?**

Say: **Put the Mighty Memory Verses inside your treasure boxes to remind you what a treasure we have in God's Word. And take a different verse out each night to see if you can remember and repeat the verse. God promises that his Word is true and will help us in every problem and place in our lives. Now let's make our own promises to God and thank him for the values he helps us grow and show in our lives.**

A POWERFUL PROMISE

Have children sit in a circle and hold their treasure boxes. Ask for a moment of silence, then say: **We've spent several weeks learning about some of the values that Jesus had in his life. We've explored love and** kindness, honesty and truth, praise and thankfulness, and forgiveness and change. And we've worked on four Mighty Memory Verses that teach us how to grow closer to God through important values.

Hold up the Bible and say: **We know that God's promises are true and that God promises to bless us if we honor, obey, and love him. Growing positive values in our lives is a good way to honor, obey, and love God. Let's make a promise of our own to God. We can each commit to seeking the values that Jesus had in his life and to putting them to work in our own lives. As we pass the Bible around our circle, we can make our own special promises. We can say, "I want to grow and show the same values Jesus had."**

Pass the Bible until everyone has had a chance to hold it. Then share a prayer thanking God for sending Jesus to love us and to teach us the values we need to have. End with a corporate "amen."

Say: **Several weeks ago we sang praise carols in the hallway for others to enjoy. Let's end our time by singing the song "Strong & Powerful" to the tune of "Jesus Loves Me."** Lead kids in singing the song two times. Encourage them to close their eyes and sing their thanks to God with still, sincere hearts.

You are strong and powerful,
Awesome Lord and wonderful.
We will sing our praise to you;
That is all we want to do.
We give you praise;
We give you praise;
We give you praise;
Our voices to you raise!

End with this responsive good-bye:
Leader: **May God's love and Jesus' values be with you.**
Children: **And also with you!**
Remind kids to take home their treasure chests. Thank children for coming and encourage them to keep their promises to God this week.

WHAT IT IS AND WHAT IT DOES

Read aloud Psalm 19:7-11. Then, using verses 7-9, fill in the spaces to reveal what God's Word is and what God's Word does for us.

PAPER DOLL PATTERN

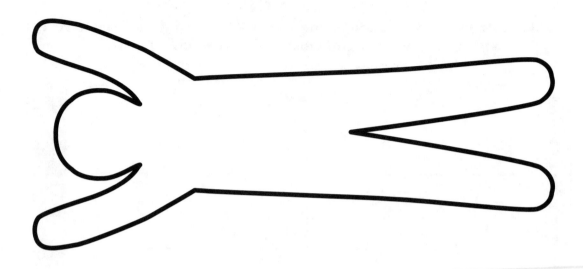

SKIT SITUATIONS

You rode your bike over the neighbors' lawn and they're upset with you. How can you show your respect? What do you do and say?

Your dad feels overworked and underappreciated. How can you show you value him? What can you do and say?

Your whispering is disturbing the boy who sits next to you in school. How can you show you respect him? What do you do and say?

You broke your brother's calculator that he kindly let you borrow. How can you show that you respect his property? What do you do and say?

You're so happy to have a best friend who sticks up for you! How can you show you value that friend? What can you do and say?

You love God and want to be even closer to him. How can you show God you value and respect him? What can you do and say?

BOOMERANG PATTERN

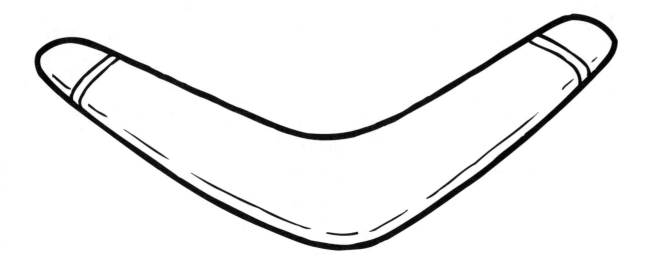

WHY DID JESUS HAVE TO DIE?

Why Did Jesus Have To Die?

Why did Jesus have to die?
To forgive me of my sins.
Jesus died so I could live
In heaven with God and him!
Thank you, Jesus!

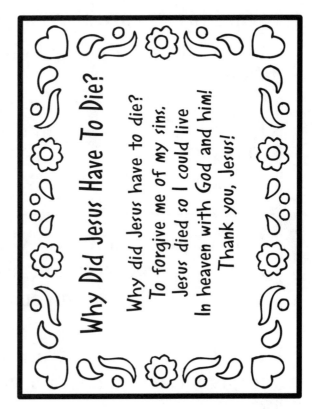

Why Did Jesus Have To Die?

Why did Jesus have to die?
To forgive me of my sins.
Jesus died so I could live
In heaven with God and him!
Thank you, Jesus!

SCRIPTURE STRIPS

Your word is a lamp to my feet and a light for my path. *Psalm 119:105*

I gain understanding from your precepts; therefore I hate every wrong path. *Psalm 119:104*

Be kind and compassionate to one another, forgiving each other, just as in Christ God forgave you. *Ephesians 4:32*

Be imitators of God, therefore, as dearly loved children and live a life of love. *Ephesians 5:1, 2a*

Enter his gates with thanksgiving and his courts with praise; give thanks to him and praise his name. *Psalm 100:4*

For the Lord is good and his love endures forever; his faithfulness continues through all generations. *Psalm 100:5*

Do not judge, and you will not be judged. Do not condemn, and you will not be condemned. Forgive, and you will be forgiven. *Luke 6:37*

In him we have redemption through his blood, the forgiveness of sins, in accordance with the riches of God's grace. *Ephesians 1:7*